BENCHMARKING STRATEGIES:

A Tool for Profit Improvement

Rob Reider, CPA, MBA, PhD
President, Reider Associates
Sante Fe, New Mexico

JOHN WILEY & SONS, INC.
New York • Chichester • Weinheim • Brisbane • Singapore • Toronto

This book is printed on acid-free paper. ∞

Copyright © 2000 by Rob Reider. All rights reserved.

Published by John Wiley & Sons, Inc.

Published simultaneously in Canada.

This publication is designed to provide accurate and authoritative information in regard to the subject matter covered. It is sold with the understanding that the publisher is not engaged in rendering legal, accounting, or other professional services. If legal advice or other expert assistance is required, the services of a competent professional person should be sought.

Library of Congress Cataloging-in-Publication Data:

Reider, Rob, 1940–
Benchmarking strategies : a tool for profit improvement / Rob Reider.
    p.   cm.
    Includes index.
    ISBN 0-471-34464-8 (alk. paper)
    1. Benchmarking (Management) I. Title.
HD62.15.R43 1999
658.5'62—dc21   99-16341
                                                                      CIP

Printed in the United States of America.

10 9 8 7 6 5 4 3 2 1

About the Author

Rob Reider, CPA, MBA, PhD, is the President of Reider Associates, a management and organizational consulting firm located in Santa Fe, New Mexico, which he founded in 1976. Prior to starting Reider Associates, he was a manager in the Management Consulting Department of Peat, Marwick in Philadelphia. His area of expertise encompasses planning and budget systems, managerial and administrative systems, computer processing, financial and accounting procedures, organizational theory, management information and control techniques, and management training and staff development.

Rob has been a consultant to numerous large, medium, and small businesses of all types in the aforementioned areas (in both the public and private sectors). In addition, he has conducted many and varied internal and external benchmarking studies and operational reviews and has trained both internal staff and external consultants in these techniques.

He is the course author and nationally sought-after discussion leader and presenter for over 20 different seminars that are conducted nationally for various organizations and associations. He has conducted more than 1,000 such seminars throughout the country and has received the AICPA Outstanding Discussion Leader of the Year award.

Rob is the course author of nine self-study courses marketed nationally. He is also the author of the professional managers handbooks titled *The Complete Guide To Operational Auditing*, 1994 and *Operational Review: Maximum Results at Efficient Costs*, 1999 published by John Wiley & Sons. He is considered a national expert in the area of performing internal and external benchmarking studies together with operational reviews.

Rob has also been a presenter at numerous professional meetings and conferences around the country and has published numerous articles in professional journals. He has also been a commentator on the educational video programs *The CPA Report, Governmental Update,* and *Accounting and Financial Managers Network* produced by Primemedia Workplace Learning.

Rob is currently listed in *Who's Who in the East, Who's Who in the West, Who's Who in the World, Who's Who in Finance and Industry, Personalities in America, International Biography, Who's Who of Emerging Leaders in America,* and so on.

Contents

Contents

Contents

Preface

All organizations, whether in the private competitive marketplace or in the public, governmental, or not-for-profit sector, owe their success to how well they understand the reasons why they are in business, their customers' needs, and how well they use their resources in their operations to produce desired results. Most organizations have a long way to go in fully achieving this understanding. Benchmarking is an effective tool to assist these organizations to obtain greater understanding.

Benchmarking is a process which analyzes and evaluates the manner in which an organization performs its functions and activities. It then compares these processes both internally to other individuals and groups and externally to other companies. Based on such comparisons, the company then identifies innovative ideas and better ways of doing things, incorporates these best practices to improve their operations and performance, and attempts to gain a competitive advantage.

Benchmarking is concerned with continuously analyzing and evaluating the company's practices through internal and external comparisons so that the company can adapt the best of these practices. For the benchmarking process to be most successful, the organization must first understand the reasons it exists, its goals, how it operates to achieve these goals, and the main processes and performance drivers (mental models and belief systems) which assist or inhibit the organization. Such organizational understanding helps the company to identify which areas of its operations to benchmark. The criteria for selecting those areas to benchmark relate to the organization's reason for existence and how critical the area is to the organization's performance toward desired results.

The organization's goals and operational requirements face constant changes, both from within the organization and outside of it. This creates ongoing opportunities, threats, constraints, and advantages. The organization must learn how to appraise and evaluate these elements of change, if it is not only to survive and meet its competition but to surpass it. Benchmarking can be an effective management and operations tool to enable an organization to achieve increased productivity and performance and accomplish its goals and desired results. With benchmarking as part of an organization's quest for best practices in a program of continuing improvements, the organization can grow and prosper; without the existence of benchmarking techniques, the organization may fall below its competitors and cease to exist.

PURPOSE AND OBJECTIVES

Benchmarking is a process that looks at how things are done in an organization in an effort to identify and implement internal and external best practices in a program of continuous improvement. It is an early warning system for operational deficiencies and the need for improvements—focusing attention on areas for improvement and operational and profit improvements. This book focuses on identifying appropriate benchmarking principles and using them effectively to improve operations and profit in any type of organization.

The objective of this book is to familiarize the reader with internal and external benchmarking principles and practices to enable the reader to develop a program of continual operational review and improvements for the organization. The goal of such an operational improvement program is to ensure that operations are conducted in the most economical, efficient, and effective manner at all times. An effective benchmarking program continually identifies present operating practices which can be improved in a program of continuous improvements—through the implementation of best practices. It is not a static or one-time project, but an ongoing organization-wide system that allows all levels of the organization to apply good common business sense and transition into an overall learning organization.

The objectives of this book in the development of such an effective organizational benchmarking program include the following:

- To increase understanding of benchmarking basics and theory: BECOMING THE BEST YOU CAN (organization, department, work unit, and so on)
- To review the benchmarking process (internal and external): HOW TO GO ABOUT IT—THE STEPS INVOLVED
- To present the process of reviewing internal operations: IDENTIFYING AREAS FOR IMPROVEMENT AND IMPLEMENTING INTERNAL BEST PRACTICES
- To increase understanding of comparing external operations—competitors, industry, and best-in-class: TO ACHIEVE THE COMPETITIVE EDGE
- To increase the ability to develop an internal program for continuous improvement as part of a learning organization: ONGOING ORGANIZATIONAL LEARNING
- To increase understanding as to how to implement, develop, and evaluate an organization's benchmarking program: FINE-TUNING THE TOOL ITSELF.

The objective of benchmarking is not to become an organizational panacea for change, but to be one of the ongoing tools for creating an effective learning organization.

CONTENTS OF BOOK

Developing an effective organizational benchmarking program includes both internal and external benchmarking concepts. It is being presented in five chapters or sections, as follows:

Chapter One: Organizational Analysis

This chapter introduces the basic concepts of benchmarking as they relate to the purposes for which organizations exist. For benchmarking to be most effective, top management must be aware of why the organization is in existence and be committed to using the best practices to make the organization the best it can be in reaching its desired goals. Top management must develop and be committed to overall organizational benchmarks which must be communicated to the rest of the organization so that all personnel are moving toward the same results. Such organizational benchmarks and goals must consider the diverse needs of various stakeholders such as the owners, management, other employees, suppliers, customers and so on.

Chapter Two: Organizational Benchmarks

For the benchmarking process to be most effective, top management must identify those organizational mental models, belief systems, and performance drivers that effect productivity and achievement of results. This chapter introduces the concept of how these organizational drivers affect the functions and activities of the organization resulting in benchmarking gaps between the organization and others. In addition, this chapter discusses the development of appropriate benchmarks for organizational growth and the identification of internal management organizational benchmarks.

Chapter Three: Internal Benchmarking

Based on the stated organizational benchmarks, the organization can then review and analyze its internal operations as to necessary best practice changes. Internal benchmarking entails the comparison of similar operations, functions, or activities within the organization to identify opportunities for improvement and best practices within a common environment. These improvement opportunities arise from one part of the company, division, work unit, or individual learning from another. This chapter discusses the ramifications of conducting an internal benchmarking study and the manner in which to conduct such a study.

Chapter Four: External Benchmarking

External benchmarking consists of comparing the organization's operations to other organizations in a formal external benchmarking study which could be one of competitive benchmarking (comparing operations to competitors), industry benchmarking (identifying trends, innovations, and new ideas within the industry), best-in-class benchmarking (looking across multiple industries to identify functional best practices) or a combination of the three. This chapter discusses external benchmarking principles, antitrust considerations, identifying quantitative and qualitative benchmarks, and choosing the appropriate benchmarking approach for the organization.

Chapter Five: External Benchmarking Process

This chapter discusses the steps necessary for conducting an effective external benchmarking study including such aspects as establishing the benchmarking team, choosing benchmark study participants, data collection procedures, development and use of external benchmarking questionnaires, interpreting and analyzing study results, identifying best practices, reporting benchmarking study results, implementing changes and so on.

> *Benchmarking Is Not a Panacea for Success,*
> *It Is a Tool to Learn Success*

CHAPTER ONE

Organizational Analysis

INTRODUCTION

Organizations have been in existence for thousands of years—some successful and long lasting, others more short-lived. Through the years there has been no clear-cut criteria or formula for success. Many business organizations have been successful through such intangible attributes as dumb luck, falling into a niche market place, being the first, consumer acceptance, and so on. Other companies using the best available business acumen and methods have failed miserably. Identifying, implementing, and maintaining the secrets of success is an elusive target. Banking on what has worked in the past and your own internal Ouija board are ineffective substitutes for objective internal appraisal and external comparison and analysis—what we call benchmarking. Benchmarking is the tool of choice for gathering data related to programs of continuous improvement and gaining competitive advantage.

Benchmarking can be defined as a process for analyzing internal operations and activities to identify areas for positive improvement in a program of continuous improvement. The process begins with an analysis of existing operations and activities, identifies areas for positive improvement, and then establishes a performance standard upon which the activity can be measured. The goal is to improve each identified activity so that it can be the best possible—and stay that way. The best practice is not always measured in terms

1

of the least costs, but may reflect what stakeholders value and expected levels of performance.

WHY ORGANIZATIONS ARE IN EXISTENCE

Before one even thinks about performing a benchmarking study of an organization, it is necessary to determine why the organization is in existence. When clients are asked this question, invariably the answer is to make money. Although this is partly true, there are really only two reasons for an organizational entity to exist:

1. *The Customer Service Business*
   To provide goods and services to satisfy desired customers, clients, patients, and so on so that they will continue to use the organization's goods and services and refer it to others.
   A successful organizational philosophy that correlates with this goal is "to provide the highest quality products and service at the least possible cost."
2. *The Cash Conversion Business*
   To create desired goods and services so that the investment in the organization is as quickly converted to cash as possible, with the resultant cash-in exceeding the cash-out (net profits or positive return on investment).

The correlating philosophy to this goal can be stated as follows: "To achieve desired organization results using the most efficient methods so that the organization can optimize the use of limited resources."

This means that we are in business to stay for the long term—to serve our customers and grow and prosper. A starting point for establishing organizational benchmarks is to decide which businesses the organization is really in so that operational efficiencies and effectiveness can be compared to such overall benchmarks.

BUSINESSES AN ORGANIZATION IS NOT IN

Once short-term thinking is eliminated, managers realize they are not in the following businesses and benchmarking decision-making becomes simpler:

- **Sales business.** Making sales that cannot be collected profitably (sales are not profits until the cash is received and all the costs of the sale are less than the amount collected) creates only numerical growth.
- **Customer order backlog business.** Logging customer orders is a paperwork process to impress internal management and outside shareholders. Unless this backlog can be converted into a timely sale and collection, there is only a future promise, which may never materialize.
- **Accounts receivable business.** Get the cash as quickly as possible, not the promise to pay. But remember, customers are the company's business; keeping them in business is keeping the company in business and normally, the company has already put out its cash to vendors and/or into inventory.
- **Inventory business.** Inventory doesn't equal sales. Keep inventories to a minimum—zero if possible. Procure raw materials from your vendors only as needed, produce for real customer orders based on agreed delivery dates, maximize work-in-process throughput, and ship directly from production when the customer needs the product. To accomplish these inventory goals, it is necessary to develop an effective organizational life stream that includes the company's vendors, employees, and customers.
- **Property, plant, and equipment business.** Maintain at a minimum: be efficient. Idle plant and equipment causes anxiety and results in inefficient use. If it is there, it will be used. Plan for the normal (or small valleys); not for the maximum (or large peaks); network to outsource for additional capacity and insource for times of excess capacity.

- **Employment business.** Get by with the least number of employees as possible. Never hire an additional employee unless absolutely necessary; learn how to cross-train and transfer good employees. Not only do people cost ongoing salaries and fringe benefits, but they also need to be paid attention, which results in organization building.
- **Management and administration business.** The more an organization has, the more difficult it becomes to manage its business. It is easier to work with less and be able to control operations than to spend time managing the managers. So much of management becomes getting in the way of those it is supposed to manage and meeting with other managers to discuss how to do this. Management becomes the promotion for doing.

If an organization does both of these successfully—if it pays attention to its business and stays out of the businesses it should not be in, it will more than likely (outside economic factors nowithstanding) grow and prosper through well-satisfied customers and keep itself in the positive cash conversion business—in spite of itself.

Of course, an organization also has to stay out of the numbers business—looking at short-term reporting criteria such as the amount of sales, backlog, locations, employees, and the big devil, "the bottom line," that others judge as success.

The organization must decide which of the above factors it wishes to embrace as organizational benchmarks, which ones it will not include as benchmarks, and which additional criteria it will include as benchmarks. These criteria become the overriding conditions on which the organization conducts its operations and against which it benchmarks.

OUTLINING BASIC BUSINESS PRINCIPLES

Each organization must determine the basic principles which guide its operations. These principles become the foundation on which the organization bases its desirable benchmarks. Examples of such business principles include the following:

- Produce the best quality product at the least possible cost.
- Set selling prices realistically, so as to sell all the product that can be produced within the constraints of the production facilities.
- Build trusting relationships with critical vendors; keeping them in business is keeping the company in business.
- The company is in the customer service and cash conversion businesses.
- Don't spend a dollar that doesn't need to be spent; a dollar not spent is a dollar to the bottom line. Control costs effectively; there is more to be made here, than by increased sales.
- Manage the company; do not let it manage the managers. Provide guidance and direction, not crises.
- Identify the company's customers and develop marketing and sales plans with the customers in mind. Produce for the company's customers, not for inventory. Serve the customers, not sell them.
- Don't hire employees unless they are absolutely needed; only when they multiply the company's effectiveness and the company makes more from them than if they did the work themselves.
- Keep property, plant, and equipment to the minimum necessary to maintain customer demand.
- Plan for the realistic, but develop contingency plans for the positive unexpected.

There seems to be an organizational trend toward empire-building, particularly from the top, and the power and control that comes with it. Even with present movements toward such things as downsizing, restructuring, reengineering, and so on, with their emphasis on getting by with less people and resources, those in power are trying to hold onto unnecessary empires of people and budget allocated resources. While management will quite agreeably

5

reduce another manager's empire, there is considerable resistance when it comes to reducing the size of their own area. In many instances, even with these quick and short-term remedies at people reductions, there still remain unnecessary (non-value added) individuals and layers of organizational hierarchy. Benchmarking, with its basic principle of doing the right thing, assists in building economic, efficient, and effective organizations, and maintaining them properly at all times using the correct techniques (best practices) for the situation. Benchmarking techniques assist the company in identifying its critical problem areas and then in treating the cause of the problems, not merely the symptoms of the problems. With sensible business principles as the hallmark for the company's benchmarking, the company can be clear as to the direction for positive movement and avoid merely improving poor practices. Clear business principles that make sense to all levels of the organization allow the company to identify and develop the proper organizational benchmarks. In this manner, everyone in the organization is moving in the same desired direction.

Here's an example of how unclear business principles get in the way of effective improvements and the implementation of best practices. I was doing some consulting work for an organization that was management top-heavy. The vice president of an operating area gave a command to the director reporting to him or her, the director in turn gave the command to one of the managers, who in turn gave it to a supervisor, who in turn gave it to a work unit chief, who gave it to a worker. I joked that the worker then gave it to the night janitor, who really did all the work in the company. When the work was done, it would go back up the pole, stopping at each point for review and then back to the employee for redo, and then finally to the vice president, who in many instances didn't need the information anymore, forgot that he or she had asked for it, or didn't understand it anyway and filed it in the circular file. If another vice president or someone reporting to him or her needed some information from this division, the request would go from vice president to vice president and then back up and down the line. I asked a number of employees how they could live with this type of organizational goings on—what I call organizational crazy-making. They didn't understand what I was talking about. I tried again by asking the employees why they did the jobs they were asked to do without questioning the need for them. I was told "we just do it, it's not our job to question." And they do it until one of them becomes a vice president.

Looking at this situation as part of the company's benchmarking efforts, this practice must be seen as a poor practice and a negative performance-driver. Rather than making it easier for employees to work and achieve the best results, this practice produces more costly, inefficient, and less than desirable results. The practice must not be considered for improvement, but as a negative organizational factor which must be overcome and eliminated. With the right basic business principles defined for the company, it will be obvious that this is a condition that must be changed rather than improved.

THE CONCEPT OF STAKEHOLDERS

Benchmarking processes are directed towards the continuous pursuit of improvement, excellence in all activities, and the effective use of best practices. The focal point in achieving these goals is the customer—both internal and external—who establishes performance expectations and is the ultimate judge of resultant quality. A company customer is defined as anyone who has a stake or interest in the ongoing operations of the organization—anyone who is affected by the results (type, quality, and timeliness). Stakeholders include all those who are dependent upon the survival of the organization, such as:

- Suppliers/vendors: external
- Owners/shareholders: internal/external
- Management/supervision: internal
- Employees/subcontractors: internal/external
- Customers/end users: external

In developing organizational benchmarks for operational performance, management needs to take into account the diverse needs

7

of each of these stakeholders. What might be best for one or more of these stakeholders might not be best for others. Management needs to balance these diverse needs in determining the best practice for the organization.

STRATEGIC CONCEPTS

Benchmarking results provide the company, owners, management, and employees, with data necessary for effective resource allocation and strategic focus in the organization. The benchmarking process provides objective measures to determine the success of the company's internal goals, objectives, and detail plans, as well as external and competitive performance measures. Benchmarking the company's performance against stakeholder expectations enables the company to pursue its program of continuous improvement and the road to excellence. Effective benchmarking encompasses both internal and external needs.

When developing organizational benchmarks through the strategic planning system, management must be fully aware of all of the factors to be considered in the development of their strategic plan. Exhibit 1.1 depicts the strategic planning and management process that considers both the external and internal organizational environment. In developing the organization's strategic plan, many factors need to be considered. Each factor may result in one or more desirable benchmarks to be integrated into the strategic plan. They are as follows:

- **Organizational mission:** why the organization is in existence, which products or services it will provide, who are its customers, what it desires to provide to each of its customers, its basic business principles upon which it will operate, and so on.
- **Organizational goals and objectives:** overall results desired to be achieved, directions to be moved toward (increase, decrease, status quo), definitions of desired best practices, critical areas for improvements.

Exhibit 1.1   Strategic Planning and Management Process

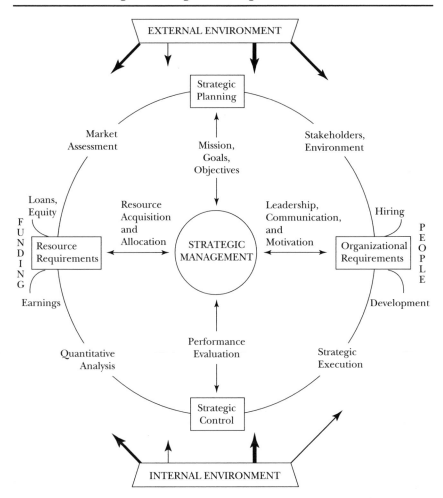

- **Stakeholders' concerns:** owners, shareholders, vendors, customers, employees, management.
- **Environmental issues:** economy (international, national, local), competitors, political, consumers, legislative conditions.
- **Organizational requirements:** personnel (hiring, training, downsizing, transferability), facilities (increase, decrease,

combine), equipment (production, data processing), systems (production, management, administrative).

- **Control and reporting systems:** identification of key operating indicators (e.g., sales by product/product line, on time deliveries, product quality, cost considerations), evaluative criteria (e.g., each late delivery), reporting format (e.g., real time online, daily summary, weekly recap), follow-up procedures.
- **Resource requirements:** personnel, facilities, equipment, funding, earnings, outside assistance, cash flow, systems.
- **Market assessment:** by product, by product line, by customer, by competitor, existing products, changes required, potential products.

An overview of the strategic planning process is shown in Exhibit 1.2. The exhibit points out some of the areas to be considered in the organization's external analysis:

- Customer analysis
- Competitive analysis
- Industry analysis
- Environmental analysis
- Opportunities, threats, and strategic questions

Exhibit 1.2 also identifies some of the internal analysis factors to consider:

- Performance analysis
- Determination of strategic options
- Strengths, weaknesses, and strategic questions

The steps in strategy identification and selection are also summarized in Exhibit 1.2.

Some strategies for competitive advantage are shown in Exhibit 1.3. These strategies can be categorized into groupings such as:

- Differentiation
- Low cost

Exhibit 1.2   Overview of the Strategic Planning Process

EXTERNAL ANALYSIS
- Customer analysis
- Competitive analysis
- Industry analysis
- Environmental analysis
  technological
  regulatory
  economic
  cultural/social
  socio-economic
  geographic
- Opportunities, threats
  and strategic questions

INTERNAL ANALYSIS
- Performance analysis
  return on investment
  market share
  product line analysis
  cost structure
  systems
  personnel capability
- Determination of
  strategic options
  past and current strategies
  strategic problems
  organizational capabilities
  and constraints
  financial resources
- Strengths, weaknesses
  and strategic questions

STRATEGY IDENTIFICATION AND SELECTION
1. Define the corporate mission
2. Identify the strategic alternatives by
   - Product or service
   - Strategic investment thrust
     growth/expansion
     stability
     retrenchment/harvest
     divestiture/liquidation
   - Functional competence
     functional area strategies
   - Unique competitive advantage
     organizational proficiency or competence
3. Select the strategy
   Consider strategic questions
   Evaluate strategic alternatives
4. Implement the strategy
   Develop operating plans
5. Review the strategies and replan as required
   Install timely and accurate information/control systems

Exhibit 1.3 Strategies for Competitive Advantage

DIFFERENTIATION	LOW COST
Quality	No-frills product
Brand name/reputation	Product design
Customer orientation	Raw material source control
Installed customer base	Government subsidy
Patent protection	Locations
Augmented protection	Product innovation/automation
Peripheral services	Own/control competitors
Technical superiority	Cost containment/low overhead
Distribution	Experience advantage
Product line breadth	Low-cost culture

COMPETITIVE
STRATEGIC
ADVANTAGE

FOCUS
Product focus
Market focus
Geographic focus
Customer focus

PREEMPTION
Service
Product
Production
Innovation
Franchising
Distribution
Supply systems
Customer loyalty

SYNERGY
Enhanced value
Reduced cost
Reduced investment
Combined resources

- Focus
- Preemption
- Synergy

Each of these strategies for competitive advantage can be applied to the entire organization, a distinct product line, a specific product, a division or department of the company, and so on. For each strategy, there may be one or more organizational benchmarks. These benchmarks are then examined for best practices to be implemented to achieve and hopefully exceed the benchmark. For example, a differentiation strategy of quality might include the following benchmarks:

- Immediate order entry into production schedule on receipt of customer order
- Vendor delivery of materials needed at time of production requirements
- Entry into production at scheduled time to ensure completion for delivery time
- Minimal time spent in production per schedule
- No excess materials, rejects, rework, scrap, production delays, and so on
- Production completed on time with total quality and correct quantity
- Shipping of order to customer on time by right method
- Billing at time of shipment (or before)—accurate and complete
- Collection from customer in timely manner (at time of shipment/receipt if possible)

EXTERNAL ORGANIZATIONAL BENCHMARKS

Some examples of external benchmarkings for the organization as an entity include the following:

- Increased sales: in total, by product line, and by product
- Earnings per share
- Total assets
- Return on investment
- Return on assets
- Gross profits
- Net profits
- Debt/equity ratio

- Stock price
- Dividends
- Cash flow changes
- Survival and growth
- Internal excellence (positive changes)
- Competitive excellence: quality, timely, cost, response
- Supplier excellence: preferred vendors
- Employer excellence: employee participation, empowerment, and so on

While owners may be most concerned with short-term benchmarking criteria such as stock market price and earnings per share, other stakeholders may be more concerned with more long-term criteria such as real earnings growth, customer satisfaction, and consistent positive cash flow. There needs to be a meaningful balance between such short-term and long-term goals of divergent stakeholders for the benchmarking process to be most successful.

CONCLUSION

The real starting point for the organizational benchmarking process is for top management to define the focus and direction desired for the organization. The initial definition is to identify the businesses that the company is in and those businesses that the company is not in. For instance, if management agrees with our concepts of being in the *customer service* and *cash conversion* businesses, they must define the parameters of what this means to them and the company. They must then do the same for the businesses they do not want to be in such as defining their concepts of the sales business, inventory business, management and administrative business, and so on. It is only through clear communication from the top to the bottom levels of the organization that everyone within the organization understands the overall organizational benchmarks.

Together with such overall business definitions, top management should also declare their basic business principles for all organizational operations. It is these basic business principles that create the framework for the identification of organizational benchmarks. It is through these organizational benchmarks that all functions and activities of the company define their desired benchmarks. In effect, an interlocking series of benchmarks is developed throughout the company which integrate with each other—from top to bottom and from bottom to top.

These organizational benchmarks consider all organizational operations as a closed loop system—each operation impacting every other one. In addition, the diverse needs of all stakeholders must be considered in the determination of the direction of the company and best practices for the organization. All of these items input into the organization's strategic planning process, so that strategic plans and thrusts as developed by senior management dovetail with the desired direction of the organization. It is within this framework that detailed organizational benchmarks are developed against which progress can be measured. It is these organizational benchmarks that provide the overall direction of the company. Organizational benchmarks, like organizational plans, must be continually reviewed.

In the next chapter, the development of such specific organizational benchmarks will be discussed. The quality of such organizational benchmarks is dependent on the time and scrutiny that top management is willing to devote to the overall organizational benchmarking process. As the organization is viewed as an integrated functional entity, the organizational benchmarking process will become more encompassing and complete.

CHAPTER TWO

Organizational Benchmarks

INTRODUCTION

With a proper strategic planning process, top management should define clear directions for all major functions and activities. Such directions should ensure that all functions are working toward the same organizational goals. The benchmarking process is a tool to help the organization to move in the correct direction by implementing (and re-implementing) best practices in an organization-wide program of continuous improvements.

In the development of organizational benchmarks, each function must be scrutinized as to its value-added contribution to the organization and the meeting of stakeholder desires and needs. The initial question is always "whether the function or activity is needed at all, and if it is, to what extent and for what purpose." Each function must be looked at in proper perspective as to its current and future need. There is no reward given for past performance. The crux is the benchmark for this function or activity at the present time—with an eye toward the necessity of the function in the future.

This chapter will discuss the principles in identifying and developing organizational benchmarks so that an effective framework is developed on which to develop such functional and activity-based benchmarks. The entire benchmarking network throughout the organization must interconnect so that all activities are focused in the same directions. It is through effective internal and external benchmarking studies that the organization and its functions are appraised as to their proximity to desired benchmarks. The conducting of internal and external benchmarking studies will be discussed in succeeding chapters. As a result of these studies, areas are identified where there is a benchmarking performance gap between actual performance and desired benchmarks. These areas are then brought up to the benchmark (then surpassing the benchmark to achieve competitive advantage) by implementing best practices in the organization's program of continuous improvements.

The development of these organizational benchmarks provides the basis on which to evaluate existing systems and procedures so as to ensure continuous efforts toward the implementation of best practices. This chapter discusses the process and principles necessary for the proper development of effective organizational principles directed toward the continual implementation of best practices. The benchmarking process should not be focused on improving functions and activities which are bad practices in themselves, but should be focused on continual analysis that allows the company to become a learning organization continually moving toward the effective achievement of desired results.

ATTRIBUTES OF BENCHMARKING/PERFORMANCE MEASURES

In developing effective organizational benchmarks, management should consider the following attributes. The development of each benchmark should be tested against these attributes prior to its establishment as an organizational benchmark:

- **Forward-looking:** considers present as well as expected future conditions
- **Holistic:** includes the needs of all stakeholders as well as those of internal functions
- **Participative:** developed and considering all stakeholders who might be affected by the benchmark
- **Quality-focused:** considers the aspects of customer service and quality considerations

18

- **Stakeholder-driven:** focuses on needs of one or more stakeholders as appropriate
- **Clear communication of goals and objectives:** all affected stakeholders know exactly what results are expected from the successful accomplishment of the benchmark
- **Identification of best practices and results:** clear description of desired best practices and the result to be accomplished through the successful implementation of the best practice
- **Ability to change to achieve best practice:** is the organization in the position to implement the necessary changes easily and effectively?
- **Part of program of continuous improvement:** is the desired benchmark and best practice part of a program of continuous improvement rather than a stand-alone benchmark?
- **Internal and competitive excellence:** is the benchmark or performance measure part of a program of internal operational and competitive excellence on an ongoing basis?

TOOLS FOR DECISION-MAKING

Organizational benchmarks provide the tools for management to make those decisions that ensure the continued growth and prosperity of the company. Such benchmarks assist in making the proper decisions in the following areas:

- **Resource allocation:** to which operational areas should the company's finite resources be allocated to achieve optimum results and overall effectiveness?
- **Strategic focus:** what strategies (e.g., quality, customer service, vendor reliability, employee productivity, and so on) will the benchmarking process address?
- **Continuous improvements:** which operational areas are considered most critical in the organization's program of continuous improvements?
- **Competitive excellence:** in which areas is the company seen to have a performance gap compared to competitors? Where

does management believe excellence needs to be maintained or improved?

- **Objective measures of success (internal and external):** what are the specific results (in quantitative measures) the benchmark should achieve?
- **Recognized levels of excellence (competitors):** what are the defined levels of excellence of your competitors and which ones do you desire to meet and then surpass?

> *Minimize Mistakes—*
> *Maximize Opportunities*

BENCHMARKS FOR ORGANIZATIONAL GROWTH

There are numerous benchmarks the organization may choose to implement in its program of continuous improvements leading toward organizational growth.

Cost Reductions

Many times, costs can be reduced or eliminated without any appreciable diminishment of the organization's efficiency or effectiveness—these cost reductions should be aggressively pursued. Other times, management is strictly looking at short-term cost reductions to puff up the company's profitability—these cost reductions should be avoided as they typically only produce short-term gain for long-term pain. Remember the principle that a dollar of cost reduction produces a dollar increase to the bottom-line net profits—but use this principle effectively.

Price Increases

Company management may decide at any time to increase the prices charged to customers for their goods and services. Such price increases may be justified in the market place (and part of a strategic plan) or just management's desire to increase revenues (hoping everything else stays the same). In this situation, a dollar increase in revenues will not produce a dollar increase in net profits. The best that can be achieved is the net profit margin of this additional sale (sales dollars less costs = net profit per sale). It is possible if the costs of this additional sale exceed the revenues generated that each additional sale results in a decrease in the bottom line. In addition, such price increases may create external competition that may cause fewer sales or incur increased costs to make each sale.

Sales Volume Increases

Part of the company's strategic plan may be to increase the level of sales to customers—both present and potential customers. It is usually easier to increase sales volumes with the company's present customers than continually to prospect for new customers. If the company has been operating efficiently, their sales personnel should be close to its customers. They should know what each customer has purchased in the past, the sales trends over a period of time by product and/or product line, what their current and future needs are, whether the company has been making an adequate profit on its sales to the customer, and so on. If such things are not known about the customer, it may be an indication of poor sales practices and a performance gap between present practices and a more desirable benchmark. Part of the company's strategic plan should be to earmark specific present customers for increased sales: what products to sell to them, at what price and what amount, and how to sell to them.

The company may also decide to increase their sales volume to potential new customers. Again, such sales plans should be incorporated into the company's organizational plan. Over-reliance upon sales to new customers may be an indication of ineffective sales and customer service procedures with existing customers, as well as costly sales practices for new customers.

Sales volume increases should always be part of overall organizational planning and integrated with other organizational functions such as sales and marketing, engineering, manufacturing, accounting, and so on.

New Market Expansion

As part of the organizational plan, the company may decide to expand its operations into new markets. It may decide to expand on a local basis, or nationally, or internationally. It could decide to introduce new products, enhance its present products, or expand the sales of its products into new markets. Each of these decisions should be part of an organized plan with its own benchmark and scheme as to how to achieve such results and the method for evaluating successful progress towards the benchmark. Such expansion may not always be positive. Management must be sure that this is the best course.

New Distribution Channels

As a benchmark for organizational growth, company management may decide to develop additional channels for marketing and distributing their products. For instance, if traditionally it has sold its products directly to customers through its own internal sales force, it may decide to use outside sales groups, sales brokers, sales representatives, and the like. Such arrangements might supplement or reinforce their inside sales efforts or might replace the internal sales force—in whole or in part. The company might also decide to distribute its products via additional distribution channels such as becoming an original equipment manufacturer (OEM), a wholesaler, a direct retailer, a mail order house, an internet seller, a direct customer seller and, so on.

Market Share Increases in Existing Markets

The organizational plan may include specific steps as to how to increase the company's market share in existing markets. The plan may include benchmarks by product line, product, or customer. Specific results should be clearly spelled out and those responsible for successful completion of each work step in the plan should be identified. The plan should be realistic and practical, the results achievable within the organization's methods of operations.

Selling or Closing a Losing Operation or Location

Sometimes an operation (product line, product, customer, etc.) or a plant or office location is deemed to be too costly in relation to the value (income or cost saving) added to the company. With the proper information, company management can arrive at the proper decision to retrench. Without such an adequate information base, management may come to the opposite conclusion—to allocate more resources into the operation or location. In this instance, management would be more than likely allocating additional expenditures to a losing proposition. Management could establish a benchmark of retrenchment, a benchmark of developing an adequate information system or both. The object of retrenchment is normally to reduce overall expenses while increasing net income—the bottom line. However, retrenchment will also decrease gross sales or income which may not be desirable to all of the stakeholders (e.g., owners or shareholders).

Acquiring Another Company, Division, Operation, or Product

Company management may decide that the quickest method for achieving a benchmark (such as increased sales, reduced costs, increased net income) is through acquisition. This could be accomplished by acquiring another company, a division of another company, a specific operation (e.g., research and development, data processing), a product line or product (e.g., a food company acquiring a complementary product), and so on. Such acquisitions should be considered using the concept of leverage. The resultant return on investment should exceed the cost of the investment. For instance, if the cost of the capital to make the acquisition is six percent, than the expected (and real) return on the investment should be sufficiently greater than six percent (e.g., over 10 percent) to cover the potential risk involved. Obtaining organizational growth through acquisition is not always positive as the company may acquire another's problems or may lack the expertise to take full advantage of the acquisition.

Developing a New Product or Service

Company management may decide that the best method to achieve organizational growth or reach a specific benchmark is to develop a new product or service. To do this effectively, the company should have a real vision of its marketplace, its existing products, its customer's requirements, the desired need for the new product, its effect on existing products, and so on. The decision to develop and market a new product should be based on integrated decisions between the company's major functions, such as sales, marketing, engineering, manufacturing, accounting, and so on.

Efficiency or Productivity Improvements

The ability either to operate more efficiently at less cost or increase productivity at the same (or less) cost may also be a workable approach to reaching a company's organizational growth benchmarks. A dollar of costs saved (all other factors remaining the same) will produce an additional dollar of earnings to the bottom line. Increasing productivity produces more of the product or service at relatively the same cost, resulting in less cost per product or service produced. Both of these approaches can be implemented and controlled by internal management and operations personnel. There is usually more to be gained in the bottom line through cost efficiencies and productivity improvements than through the various methods of revenue or sales enhancements discussed above. Remember that a dollar in sales increase does not add a dollar to the bottom line, only the incremental amount of net income generated by the additional sale which could be a loss. Cost efficiencies and productivity improvements are two of the major areas to be considered in an internal benchmarking study as part of the company's program of continuous improvements and best practices.

Non–Value-Added Activities Eliminated

Functions or activities which add no value to the product or service should be eliminated. As part of the benchmarking study, such functions or activities should be identified. Company management should be able to identify those areas to be benchmarked for elimination. For instance, they may identify all unnecessary quality control inspections or the preparation of purchase orders. Or they may benchmark the desirability of eliminating an entire function, such as raw material storekeeping or credit and collections. This establishes the focus for those areas to be considered in a benchmarking study. The study team can identify best practices and the most efficient methods for eliminating such functions or activities. They can also consider the resultant ramifications to remaining operations after the reduction or elimination of these non-value added functions or activities. Typically, there is a multiplier effect, that is the elimination or reduction of one activity results in similar reductions or elimination of other activities.

> ## *Increase Value Without Sacrificing Interests of Any Stakeholders*

Making Employees Responsible

Make employees responsible for meeting company expectations and results through motivating self-disciplined behavior. With an effective monitoring system, this eliminates the need for management personnel to exist mainly for policing and controlling these individuals—with minimal value-added activities. Use of operating systems that make sense to the workers (where they have had input in developing such systems), who use them within a working-together atmosphere (rather than a working-for atmosphere) will increase productivity to the extent that fewer employees overall are needed. The trick is not to bring on unnecessary personnel as the company grows, so that the company is never in a position to have to cut back drastically. Many times a company penalizes the individuals being downsized or laid off for something out of their control. Benchmarking helps to keep the company in focus regarding the types and levels of personnel required at any time.

Organizational Structure Revisions

There are many techniques for building an organization structure which are not dependent on the typical top-to-bottom military model based on policing and controlling those reporting to each higher level. Some other techniques for organizational structure include participative management, shared management, team management, self-motivated disciplined behavior (no manager), coaching and facilitative supports, and so on. There is no right answer for all situations. The company must learn to use a combination of these techniques as they fit the particular situation. The benchmarking process allows the company to achieve the best organizational structure overall, as well as within each function and activity. Benchmarking emphasizes controlling results, not people, fixing the cause not the blame, and doing the *right* job right not just doing the job right.

BENCHMARKING PRINCIPLES

Benchmarking is the comparison of existing practices in your organization to best practices used elsewhere (within the company or outside of the company), used as a management tool for change. The first step in identifying those areas for benchmarking is to fully understand each function in the organization by answering questions relating to each function:

- What is its purpose?
- Why is it being done?
- How is it being done?
- By whom is it being done?
- What does it cost to get it done and is it cost-effective?
- Does it add value to our product or service?
- Is it achieving desired results?
- Can it be done less costly?
- Can it be done more productively?
- Can it be reduced or eliminated?

- Is there a better "best practice"?
- Can it be combined, simplified, or made more efficient?

Some of the functions that should be considered include the following:

- Customer service and relations (customer service functions)
- Sales and marketing (selling functions)
- Cash receipts and disbursements (cash conversion functions)
- Credit and order entry (administrative functions)
- Purchasing, accounts payable, payment (support functions)
- Ship/deliver (customer delivery functions)
- Bill, accounts receivable, collections (accounting functions)

As part of considering the functions for organizational benchmarking, company management should identify:

- Opportunities for improvement (to become the best that the company can)
- Gaps in performance (where the company is compared to where it wants to be)
- Best practices—both internal and external (where the company can gain sustainable competitive advantage)

Identifying those areas or functions to benchmark within the organization and establishing benchmark and best practice targets trigger:

- Quality programs
- Cost reduction efforts
- Planning and budget process realities
- Operational review improvement programs
- Management and organizational changes
- New operations and ventures

- Rethinking existing strategies
- Competitive assaults

Strive for Perfection—Settle for Excellence

Many organizations have developed systems which they consider helpful, such as planning, budgeting, compensation, reporting, cost control, and so on. These systems, rather than being helpful, may result in the accumulation of unnecessary staff and resources, characterized by multi-tiered organization levels and excessive budgets and expenditures. As an example, while some companies are reducing staff size through downsizing and cost cutting, they are hiring new employees at the same time. When the company reduces staff size, are they asking the right questions such as:

- Are we getting rid of the right people?
- Why were they hired in the first place?
- How did they get to these positions?
- How effective are our hiring, orientation, training, evaluation, and promotion practices?
- What is our promotion criteria? Is it effective?
- What are the causes of our organizational problems? How can we correct them?
- What organizational structure should work best for us? For the company and each work area?
- Are there areas in the company where we actually need additional personnel?
- Do we need the function at all?
- Can we achieve the same or better results in another manner (e.g., outsourcing, contractors, part-timers, staff as needed, and so on)?

- What do we do from here? Are we any smarter after downsizing and cost-cutting?
- How do we keep improvements (best practices) on a continuing basis?

The effective use of benchmarking principles helps the company to answer all of these questions, as well as many others which may surface in the company's continual efforts at implementing best practices and improvements.

TYPES OF BENCHMARKING

Benchmarking has come to be known as a comparative process—comparing performance or results of one individual or group to another. The benchmarking process for an organization should start with management's identification, and clear communication, of the direction and focus of the company, both long- and short-term. The next step is for management to define their benchmarks for organizational growth. With such direction from top management, others in the organization can then develop their corresponding benchmarks for individuals, activities, functions, departments, and so on. Departmental management and operations personnel can then analyze their activities to develop best practices in a program of continuous improvements. Such analysis is usually done first in an internal benchmarking study, enabling the operation to become the best it can from within, and then if desired through an external benchmarking study which provides for comparison to other organizations.

Internal Benchmarking

Analysis of existing practices within various operating areas of the company identifies activities, drivers, and best performance. Drivers are the causes of work or triggers (e.g., customer order) that set in motion a series of activities. Internal benchmarking focuses on looking at the company itself before looking externally at other companies. Significant positive improvements can be made as management question such things as:

- Is that activity needed?
- Why does the company (or department or work unit) do that?
- Is that function or position or material really needed?
- Can the activity be done better in another manner?
- Is that step necessary? Does it provide value added?

Internal benchmarking is the first step in benchmarking because it provides the framework to improve internal operations to best practices prior to comparing internal practices to external best-practice benchmark data. Internal benchmarking can be accomplished solely within the control of the organization. It requires no outside participation. Internal benchmarking principles and suggested steps for performing an internal benchmarking study will be discussed in Chapter 3.

External Benchmarking

External benchmarking consists of comparing company operations to other organizations in some kind of formal study such as the following.

Competitive Benchmarking. Looks to the outside to identify how other direct competitors of the company are performing. Competitive benchmarking identifies the strengths and weaknesses of the company's competitors—helpful in determining the company's own successful competitive strategy. It can also help to prioritize specific areas for improvement such as customer service, operating efficiencies, cost data, performance results, and so on.

Industry Benchmarking. Extending beyond the typical one to one comparison of competitive benchmarking, industry benchmarking attempts to identify trends, innovations, and new ideas within the company's specific industry. Such identification can help to establish better performance criteria, but may not lead to competitive breakthroughs. Remember that others in the industry may be going through the same benchmarking process as the company. The benchmarking process is thus continual.

Best-in-Class Benchmarking. Looks across multiple industries to identify new, innovative practices—regardless of their source. This search for best practices should be the ultimate goal of the benchmarking process. It supports continuous improvement, increased performance levels, and movement towards best practices, and identifies opportunities for positive improvements. Best-in-class benchmarking could be done for a specific function such as purchasing, accounts payable, data processing, and the like, or for an organizational system such as planning, budgeting, organizational structure, and so on.

External benchmarking principles and the steps in conducting an external benchmarking study will be discussed in Chapters 4 and 5.

THE BENCHMARKING PROCESS

The benchmarking process begins by looking at where the company is at the present moment in the various areas identified for benchmarking. Each of these areas is then appraised as to where the company would like to be in the future—that is the benchmark for performance. The difference between where the company is and where they would like to be is called the *benchmark gap*. The company should then develop a plan (e.g., an internal benchmarking study, an external benchmarking study, an implementation effort) to close the benchmark gap—and ultimately to surpass the benchmark.

The benchmarking process and the concept of the benchmark gap is shown in Exhibit 2.1. Note that the identified benchmark is constantly changing; deciding to stand still actually is losing ground for the company. Also, the larger the benchmark gap between where the company is and where they want to be, the more critical the specific benchmarked area. This is extremely important in deciding which areas to include in an internal and/or external benchmarking study. Should there be a large positive benchmark gap in the

Exhibit 2.1 Benchmarking Process and the Benchmark Gap

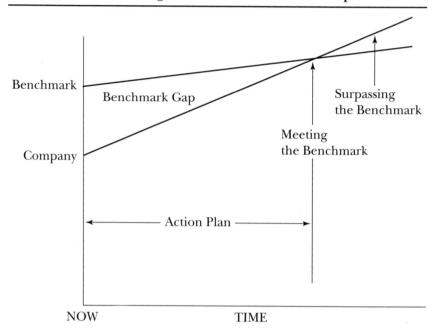

RULES:
1. The benchmark is constantly changing.
2. Standing still = losing ground = freefall to oblivion.
3. The goal is to meet and then exceed benchmark.
4. Larger the benchmark gap = more critical.
5. Large positive gap in your favor = high competitive advantage to exploit.

> ## *It Is the Customer's Perspective Not Management's That Is Key*

company's favor, this represents a high competitive advantage to exploit. In all cases, the company's goal should be to not just meet the benchmark, but to work on continually exceeding the benchmark.

BENCHMARKING PROCESS STEPS

As discussed above, the starting point for organizational benchmarking should be management's identification of benchmarks for organizational growth. Based on these top management organizational benchmarks, other management and operations personnel should develop their departmental, work unit, or individual functional benchmarks which correspond to the organizational benchmarks set by top management. In this manner, all of the personnel within the organization are working toward the same benchmarks and results for the company. It is then management's responsibility to ensure that the company progresses toward these benchmarks. It is through internal and external benchmarking studies that the organization redefines its benchmarks and best practices in its program of continuous improvements. The identification of organizational benchmarks is a continual process as management and operations personnel identify their processes and activities as a learning organization. The process steps to be considered in benchmark identification include:

- Identification of core issues and critical areas for improvements
- Detailing the work flow and process steps
- Questioning each function, activity, or work step
- Data collection
- Analyzing and interpreting the information
- Implementing the best practice

Identification of Core Issues and Critical Areas for Improvement

Many of these areas are already known, others need to be identified. Such identification can be accomplished through some form of communication or brainstorming between management and operations personnel. Typically, management has a general idea of which operational areas are most critical and in need of improvement as evidenced by a wide benchmark gap between present operations and desired levels of performance.

33

Operations personnel, however, may have an in-depth knowledge of the specific critical area, what is and isn't working, and what needs to be done to make the operation more efficient and effective. It is the blending of management and operations personnel knowledge that enhances the clear identification of the company's critical areas for improvement.

Detailing the Workflow and Process Steps

Quite often, functions and processes are conducted repetitively within an organization, without anyone ever questioning the operation:

- Why the operation is being performed?
- Who is performing the operation? Which personnel and how many?
- Why the operation is done that way?
- What results are expected through the performance of the operation?
- Can the entire operation or certain work steps be eliminated or reduced?

Analysis of the work flow—work step by work step—can help answer these questions. A good tool for accomplishing this analysis is a systems or process flowchart. Such a flowchart provides a graphic presentation of each work step in the process. This enables company personnel to question the necessity of each work step and whether it can be accomplished more economically and efficiently. As each work step is analyzed and detailed, it is scrutinized as to the above questions and others. When deficient practices are identified, they are considered for elimination or correction. This can become the starting point for identifying best practices either from within the organization or externally from others. The systems flowchart could then be redone for the same operation showing the incorporation of best practices and related improvements in economy, efficiency, and effectiveness.

Questioning Each Function, Activity, or Work Step

As part of the analysis of each operational area, the individual function, activity, or work step should be questioned as to its usefulness. For instance, why is it done in the first place? Is there a value-added need to the providing of the product or service—from a customer service or cash conversion basis? Or is the activity performed from a non–value-added basis simply because that is the way we've always done it? Can the work step be performed more economically, efficiently, or effectively? Can it be done in a better fashion—is there a better practice?

Data Collection

Together with analyzing and detailing the system or process flow, it is also important to determine the extent of the operation, involving such questions as:

- How often is the process performed? Continually, daily, weekly?
- How long does the process take? Seconds, minutes, hours?
- What does it cost?
- What is the volume of transactions?
- What is the cost of each transaction?
- What are the activities or work steps that make up the transaction?
- What functions and personnel are involved in the process? How many?
- What is the quality of the process? Number of good transactions, rejected transactions, corrected or reworked transactions?
- What is the timeliness of the processing and completion of the process or transaction? On-time completion, late completion, early completion?

To assist in developing such data, there are various tools such as transaction logs (by function or by individual), internal survey or questionnaire forms, counting systems (e.g., number of purchase orders processed), computer produced totals, and so on.

For comparison purposes, a benchmark questionnaire could be used—internally within the company to compare individuals or work units performing the same function or externally to compare the company with others such as competitors, industry, or functionally (best in class comparison).

Analyzing and Interpreting the Information

After the system and related data is fully analyzed and understood, the information must be interpreted. For instance, what work steps in the process will remain as is (where the company has the best practice), what work steps will be eliminated (it is unnecessary, non-value-added, or redundant), and what work steps will be improved (where a best practice exists elsewhere—internally within the company or from somewhere outside the company). Based on such interpretation, it can be determined that some action must be taken to correct these situations:

• The process costs too much
• The process takes too long
• The process is inefficient (e.g., unwieldy work steps)
• The process is ineffective (e.g., results not being achieved)
• Quality is poor (e.g., too many rejects)
• Unacceptable levels of customer service
• Inadequate timeliness of cash conversion
• The process is unnecessary
• The process is a duplication or redundant

As an area is identified for improvement, it is helpful to determine the existing benchmark gap between where the company practice is at present and where it is desired to be (initially to match internal and external competitors and then to surpass them). This becomes the quest for the best practice in a program of continuous improvement. Sometimes the best practice is readily identifiable (by employees, outside consultants, or through comparisons to other organizations), while other times additional research or study must be done.

Implementing the Best Practice

The desired best practice should be clearly identified in consort with management's organizational benchmarks. Once a best practice has been identified and agreed on by both management and operations personnel, an implementation plan must be properly developed. Operations personnel usually accomplishes this best, with management's approval. Both parties must be clear as to what is versus what should be—that is the desired benchmark.

Normally, the process doesn't stop with the implementation of the best practice. Management will redefine its organizational benchmarks (on a continual basis) and operational personnel will analyze and review their operations as part of a program of continuous improvements. Everyone within the organization should learn from the process so that the company becomes a learning organization. Benchmarking is not a one time effort, but continues all the time.

MENTAL MODELS AND BELIEF SYSTEMS

Many organizations operate on the basis of prevalent mental models or belief systems—usually emanating from past and present top management. These mental models and belief systems have an overriding effect on the conditions with which operations within the company are carried out. They can help to produce a helpful working environment or atmosphere, or a hindering one. In effect, such mental models become performance drivers—those elements within the organization that shape the direction of how employees will perform their functions. Examples of such mental models and belief systems include the following:

- Hard work and doing what you are told are the keys to success for the individual and the company.

- The obedient child in the company survives and is promoted, while the rebellious child is let go or leaves the company.
- Only managers can make decisions.
- Power rises to the top—and stays there.
- Employees need to be watched to do their jobs.
- Power and control over employees is necessary to get results.
- Managers are responsible, employees are basically irresponsible.
- Those at the top of the organization know what they are doing.
- All functions should be organized in the same manner.
- Higher levels of organization ensure that lower levels do their jobs.
- Policing and control over employees ensures their compliance.
- All employees are interchangeable.
- Doing the job right is more important than doing the right job.
- Control the people, control the results.
- Organizational position is more important than being right.
- Top management has the right to set all policies and procedures.
- Managers create results—employees do the job.
- Organizational hierarchies ensure that things get done.
- Employees can not be trusted on their own.
- You can not run a business without the proper organization structure.
- Managers know more than employees.
- Managers have a right to be obnoxious.
- Management is the enemy.
- Each function needs its own organization structure.
- The more employees reporting to you (and the larger your budget), the more important you are within the organization.

The accurate identification of organizational mental models, belief systems, and performance drivers is extremely important in the company's benchmarking strategy. If these things are not changed, best practice changes will only change the system and not company results.

An example of an organizational mental model, how it gets in the way, and how to remove it as a negative performance driver is as follows. We were performing an organization study for a fairly sizable food processor to determine whether the present organization structure was the most efficient for the company. Company management was concerned about the spiraling upward costs of personnel, especially the number of long-term employees and the increasing number of supervisors and managers. Top management believed that they were not getting the increased level of productivity that the company was paying for. In effect, they believed that the same amount of work was being spread out among a larger number of employees. There was an acute problem of over-organization in the headquarters office area and they asked us to start our study there.

We interviewed and observed operations in a number of the office areas such as personnel, purchasing, accounting, data processing, sales, and so on. In all of these areas, the same pattern was detected: levels of supervision and management without much value-added work and the employees competing to become a supervisor or manager. The prevalent mental model was to recognize promotion to a supervisory or management position as a reward for past service and permission to stop working—to merely review what those employees reporting to them had done and to return it for redo.

As a result of this mental model, the employees in these departments were spending more time trying to impress their bosses with fancy footwork leading toward promotion rather than just doing the actual work. Much of this was due to the mental model creating a negative performance driver of the practice of incremental annual pay increases (e.g., 5% increases), while a management promotion produced a geometric pay increase (e.g., doubling salary level in three years). The company held the belief system that this practice made their employees more competitive with each other, increasing individual productivity and providing them with better managers. In reality, this system produced employees who knocked each other out to get to the boss to show what they had done and at the same time talk down the work of the other employees. More time was being spent on impressing the boss than on doing the work. This resulted in more employees needed to do the work that wasn't getting done. Productivity was not increased and more employees were hired to do the same work (and in some cases even less work). With all of the impressing of bosses, there were more employees singled out for promotion which resulted in the unnecessary increase of supervisory and management positions.

To turn this detrimental belief system around and turn a vicious circle into a virtuous circle, we recommended that the company implement a system of individual employee expectations and results. The employee would be rewarded based on the achievement of results and not by promotion to manager. We wanted not only to eliminate the present belief system, mental model, and negative performance, but to replace it with a best practice that would meet management's desired organizational benchmark of a more efficient organizational structure. The best practice recommendation placed the burden of productivity on the employee and eliminated the need for managers to police and control employees. The employees would police and control themselves. It also eliminated the competition between employees to curry the favor of the boss as each employee was now competing against him or herself and his or her expected results. Compensatory rewards were now tied to individual performance results, which immediately increased productivity and reduced the need for as many employees and managers. Employees also felt more relaxed and comfortable as they didn't have to impress a boss and could concentrate on what they did best— their work. Eliminating the mental model of competing for promotion to management created a best practice of working together and cooperation.

INTERNAL ORGANIZATIONAL BENCHMARKS

As previously discussed, the first step in successful benchmarking is to define the company's organizational benchmarks as related to its reasons for existence, basic business principles, mental models, belief systems, performance drivers, and so on. These internal organizational benchmarks typically encompass the organization as an entity as well as its major functions. An example of such an organizational benchmarking structure is as follows:

Organization-Wide Benchmarks

- Operate all activities in the most economical, efficient, and effective manner as possible.
- Provide the highest-quality products to our customers at the least possible cost.
- Satisfy our customers so that they will continue to use the company's products and refer the company to others.
- Convert the cash invested in the business as quickly as possible so that the resultant cash in exceeds the cash out to the greatest extent possible.
- Achieve desired results using the most efficient methods so that the company can optimize the use of limited resources.
- Maximize net profits without sacrificing quality of operations, customer service, or cash requirements.

Sales Function

- Make sales to the right customers which can be collected profitably.
- Develop realistic sales forecasts which result in a present or future real customer order.
- Sell those products as determined by management to the right customers, at the right time, in the right quantities.
- Actual customer sales should directly correlate with management's long- and short-term plans.
- Sales efforts and corresponding compensation systems should reinforce the goals of the company.
- Customer sales should be integrated with other functions of the company, such as manufacturing, engineering, accounting, purchasing, and so on.

Manufacturing

- Operate in the most efficient manner with the most economical costs.
- Integrate manufacturing processes with sales efforts and customer requirements.
- Manufacture in the most timely manner considering processes such as customer order entry, timely throughput, and customer delivery.
- Increase productivity of all manufacturing operations on an ongoing basis.
- Eliminate, reduce, or improve all facets of the manufacturing operation including receiving, inventory control, production control, storeroom operations, quality control, supervision and management, packing and shipping, maintenance, and so on.
- Minimize the amount of resources such as personnel, facilities, and equipment which are allocated to the manufacturing process.

Personnel

- Provide only those personnel functions which are absolutely required as value-added activities.
- Maintain the levels of personnel at the minimum level required to achieve results in each functional area.
- Provide personnel functions such as hiring, training, evaluation, and firing in the most efficient and economical manner possible.
- Develop an organizational structure that organizes each function in the most efficient manner for their purposes.
- Minimize the hiring of new employees by such methods as cross-training and inter-departmental transfers and other best practices.
- Implement compensation systems that provide for effective employee motivation and the achievement of company goals.

Purchasing

- Purchase only those items where economies can be gained through a system of central purchasing.
- Implement direct purchase systems for those items that the purchasing function does not need to process, such as low-dollar purchases and repetitive purchases.
- Simplify systems so that the cost of purchasing is the lowest possible.
- Effectively negotiate with vendors so that the company obtains the right materials at the right time at the right quality at the right price.
- Maintain a vendor analysis system so that vendor performance can be objectively evaluated.
- Develop effective computerized techniques for economic processing, adequate controls, and reliability.

Accounting

- Analyze the necessity of each of the accounting functions and related activities, such as accounts receivable, accounts payable, payroll, budgeting, and general ledger.
- Operate each of the accounting functions in the most economical manner.
- Implement effective procedures which result in the accounting functions more analytical than mechanical.
- Develop computerized procedures that integrate accounting purposes with operating requirements.
- Develop reporting systems that provide management with the necessary operating data and indicators which can be generated from accounting data.
- Eliminate or reduce all unnecessary accounting operations that provide no value-added incentives.

The development of such organizational benchmarks provides the basis on which to evaluate current practices, identify critical problem areas, analyze detailed operations, identify best practices, and implement solutions in a program of continuous improvements. Without the definition and communication of such organizational benchmarks, the company's benchmarking efforts may only succeed in developing best practices for functions and activities that in themselves are bad practices. Benchmarking should not be an effort to improve bad practices, but to develop procedures which bring best practices into the organization. Through the benchmarking process, operating functions and activities are evaluated as to their necessity as related to the achievement of organizational goals and objectives. If a function or activity is not necessary, it should be eliminated. If it is needed, it should be considered for improvement, looking for the best present practice, and continually analyzed in the company's program of continuous improvements. Through this process, the company starts to develop itself as a learning organization, with individuals responsible for their own results. The benchmarking process becomes an ongoing integral tool, allowing the company to do things the right way and to keep doing them that way.

CONCLUSION

Organizations should be set up so that each individual, from the highest to the lowest levels, can flourish and move toward his or her real potential. A healthy organization is characterized by people working together, rather than working for atmosphere and a cooperative rather than a competitive environment. Individuals should know clearly what is expected of them and management should hold them accountable for achieving the agreed on results. Employees should work in a self-motivated, disciplined behavior modality.

This is wonderful theory and wish fulfillment if all organizations operated in this manner. If it is the goal of the company to become such a healthy organization, the benchmarking process can help it achieve this. Why can't all organizations achieve these benchmarks with all of the other management systems such as total quality management, reengineering, reinventing, restructuring, and so on that have come down the pike over the years? The answer is that people in organizations, especially in a management-is-status philosophy, get in their own way. Basic respect for the individual is so undermined that the employees spend more time playing internal gotcha games than doing what's right. Benchmarking is a system that looks at all aspects of the organization to enable the organization to do the right thing and keep doing it that way.

Organizations tend to operate based on company policies, established by top management. These policies establish the tone or atmosphere for the organization to conduct its business. They become the mental models, belief systems, and performance drivers of the organization. For instance, policies may set up a loose framework of operations such as site- or departmental-based management (each company segment operates its own way), or a tightly controlled management structure which might require all expenditures over a certain amount (e.g., $1,000) to be approved by headquarters management. Top management may see its turf as the right to establish policies over those they employ. Sometimes these policies are formally written and may be enshrined in oppressive tomes sent down from the mountain of officialdom, or they may be informal as the troops interpret the whims of top management. The benchmarking process attempts to diffuse the negative impact such policies may have on the organization and replace them with what is right for the situation.

If employees knew exactly what was expected of them, were properly oriented and trained (e.g., through a coaching and facilitative process), and were objectively evaluated and rewarded based on their accomplishment of results, organizations might have a chance of operating smoothly and becoming successful. However, those running organizations may be their own worst enemies when they create atmospheres that encourage what I call organizational nonsense, rather than an atmosphere of effective problem-solving and doing the right thing. As part of the organizational appraisal of the benchmarking process, the company should look at those organizational goings-on that really don't impact the achievement of results. It is these things that need to be changed if the benchmarking process is to be successful. The next step is an internal benchmarking study.

CHAPTER THREE

Internal Benchmarking

INTRODUCTION

Once the organization has fully defined its desired organizational benchmarks for the company as a whole and for each department, function, and activity; has identified and communicated its basic business principles to all company personnel; and has developed sound long- and short-term plans throughout the organization; they are ready to review and analyze internal operations by conducting an internal benchmarking study. Internal benchmarking entails the comparison of similar operations, functions, or activities within an organization to identify opportunities for improvement and best practices within a common environment. For an organization to maximize the benefits from internal benchmarking, it is best to fully understand and document its existing systems and procedures. Such internal benchmarking steps help to identify critical areas of the company's activities, related performance drivers, and opportunities for positive improvements. These improvement opportunities arise from one part of the company, division, work unit, or individual learning from another. In this manner, overall communication processes improve, areas of excellence are identified, and operating procedures change to reflect best practices.

In the internal benchmarking study, the study team analyzes and reviews those activities that make up the critical operational area for improvement. The study team can consist of all company employees—from management and operations from the areas under study and/or from other areas of the company—or a combination of internal personnel and outside consultants. It is extremely important that the company considers who is included in the study team as the review of operations and resultant best practice recommendations are a direct correlation to the background, experience, and expertise of the members of the study team. Typically, the study team will address two major areas of the operation—people and operating procedures. Some questions that the study team should ask as part of the internal benchmarking study relative to people and operating procedures are shown in Exhibit 3.1.

Exhibit 3.1   Internal Benchmarking Questions

A. PEOPLE

1. Who is involved? And why?
   - Number of people
   - Number of positions
   - How organized and managed
   - Current personnel resource demands
2. Are all personnel needed?
   - Reasons for involvement
   - What are they doing
   - Value- or non-value-added
   - Vital operation or task
   - Special expertise
3. Responsibility for outcomes?
   - Hierarchical pyramid: power and control
   - Management oriented: review and redo
   - Employee self-motivated disciplined behavior
   - Delegation of authority to lowest operational levels
   - Empire building: work continues—reason no longer valid

B. OPERATING PROCEDURES

1. Why task is performed? (It's always been done this way)
2. Necessary or unnecessary? (That's the way we do it)
3. Adding value to customer? (internal vs. external viewpoint)

Exhibit 3.1 *(Continued)*

---

4. Unnecessary bureaucracy? (unwieldy hierarchy)
5. Ineffective, inefficient, or redundant procedures?
6. What does each one do and why does the employee do it? (foundation for internal improvements)
7. What are the bundles or groups of value- and non-value-added procedures and activities?

Work Is Performance Art

Management, operations personnel, and members of the internal benchmarking team should be aware of the benefits such an internal benchmarking study can point out. Such awareness is important to ensure commitment from all of the parties involved in the internal benchmarking study. A list of some of the internal benchmarking benefits are shown in Exhibit 3.2.

Exhibit 3.2   Internal Benchmarking Benefits

---

1. Defines existing processes and activities and establishes baseline of acceptable performance. This helps to trigger continuous improvement efforts.
2. Identifies gaps in performance in similar internal processes. This provides a clear picture of the organization's problems.
3. Brings all internal operations up to the highest possible level of performance within existing constraints.
4. Identifies areas of internal operational improvements without going outside the organization. This eliminates the need for external benchmarking.
5. Establishes standards for common practices and procedures. This overcomes the "not-created-here" syndrome.
6. Opens up communication lines within the organization. This focuses resources on problems affecting more than one area.
7. Establishes organization-wide commitment to benchmarking. This recasts the problems facing the company.

(continues)

49

Exhibit 3.2   *(Continued)*

8. Establishes ground work for external benchmarking efforts. This ensures greater results when external benchmarking is done.
9. Prioritizes critical areas for benchmarking opportunities. This develops best practices in a program for continuous improvements.
10. Identifies and classifies the key performance drivers. This allows for changes in mental models and belief systems.

> ### *You Cannot Mandate, Only Suggest, Results Are Up to Others*

INTERNAL BENCHMARKING PROCESS

The internal benchmarking process typically starts with the identification of critical areas where positive improvements can provide maximum results. Often, such critical areas are identified in the process of organizational benchmarking, development of organizational long- and short-term plans, definition of the company's basic business principles, and so on. In addition, during this initial process, a number of functions and activities may be identified that can be resolved without inclusion in a formal internal benchmarking study. For instance, these functions or activities may be eliminated, reduced, or improved through the implementation of a best practice without the need for further study. In most organizations, the 80/20 rule applies: 20 percent of all activities result in 80 percent of the organization's ineconomies, inefficiencies, and ineffectiveness; and 80 percent of the activities result in 20 percent of their problems. Therefore, internal benchmarking study efforts should focus on those activities that constitute 20 percent of the company's most critical areas—chase the elephants not the mice. The remaining 80 percent of activities should be handled by internal operations staff as part of the program of continuous improvement.

Top management may be able to identify a number of these critical areas on their own or through the process of developing organizational benchmarks, plans, and basic business principles. The process itself forces management to analyze all aspects of company operations. As they compare each operation, function, or activity they need to look at its strengths and weaknesses and determine what is working well and what is not. Through this process, management identifies those critical areas they believe should be analyzed in greater depth in an internal benchmarking study. It is good practice to include lower levels of management as well as operations personnel in this process, as these personnel typically have greater insight into operational concerns and what needs to be done to correct any faulty practices than those management personnel at the top of the organization. This allows for more accurate identification of critical operational problem areas and the immediate or short-term improvement of these areas. This results in including only the most critical areas in the internal benchmarking study and correcting those deficiencies prior to the study.

In addition, the company's mental models, belief systems, and performance drivers can be considered by top management, other levels of management and supervision, and operations personnel. With an effective top to bottom, and bottom to top communication system during this front-end process, the organization can reduce or eliminate many of these items prior to the study. Those negative mental models, belief systems, or performance drivers can also change prior to extensive internal benchmarking efforts. At the least, these items can be brought to management and operations personnel's attention so that effective dialogue can begin as to the adverse effects of these items and what, if anything, can be done about them.

In effect, it is incumbent upon the organization to identify and clean up all operating factors that cause negative results or prevent the operational area from progressing toward a desired benchmark or closing a known benchmark gap. Prior to the beginning of the internal benchmarking study, the company should strive to have all of its operating activities in the best shape possible based solely on their knowledge of the company's operations. Management and operations personnel can make these changes themselves or work with the internal benchmarking team to make such changes. These areas may also be included in the internal benchmarking study for further best practices and improvements.

During this process, the company may also identify gaps in performance, results, reporting systems, organization, operating systems, and so on. As these gaps are identified, company management together with operations personnel may identify the dimensions of the gap, the cause (not the symptom) of the gap, and an immediate or short-term best practice solution. Appropriate steps should correct these gaps immediately. There is no need to wait for the results of the internal benchmarking study. However, as part of the internal benchmarking study, even better practices may be identified for these areas, which should then replace the previously implemented best practices. In addition, management and operations personnel should still consider any area improved in this manner through a best practice in the company's ongoing program of continuous improvements.

It is the responsibility of all company personnel, management and operations, continually to improve their area of responsibility and operation. Such a program of improvements and best practices goes on continuously, before the internal benchmarking study, during the study, and after the study. Theoretically, the internal benchmarking study is not a one-time study but an ongoing process. The study itself may provide the organization with a proper starting point as to best practices relative to economical, efficient, and effective operations. However, it is the responsibility of all company personnel to do the right thing at all times—and keep it that way. In this manner, all personnel continually review operations, best practices are continually updated, and the company's program of continuous improvements produces optimum results.

While there is no precise way in which to conduct an internal benchmarking study for all organizations, there are certain guidelines as to how to conduct such a study. It is incumbent on the internal benchmarking team to decide which work steps and procedures to include in their specific study based on the organization and the functional areas to be reviewed. The time allotted to such a study would also be a factor of the scope of the organization and the functions to be reviewed, as well as the size of operations.

An overview of the internal benchmarking process is shown in Exhibit 3.3.

Exhibit 3.3   Internal Benchmarking Process Overview

- Review of physical conditions
  Plant and office layout—ineffective working conditions
  Overcrowding conditions
  Too much space for limit of activities
  Inadequate or improper equipment or materials
  Under or over capacity
  Poor work distribution and routing
  Over-extravagant for functions being performed

- Review of functional activities
  Who is involved? Number, levels, organization, type, functions
  Why are they involved? Responsibility, authority, function, value-/non–value-added, redundant, multiple effectiveness, special expertise, necessary for action
  What are they doing? Material and supplies needed, activities performed, reformatting, enhancing, value-added activities, communicating
  Why are they doing it? That's the way we do it, always done this way, directed by supervision or management, control purposes, necessary value added

- Identify value and non-value-added activities
  Is function or activity necessary for the providing of the product or service?
  Does the product or service benefit from the activity performed?
  Can the cost of the activity justifiably be charged back to the customer as part of the production process?
  Is the activity considered part of non-productive overhead costs?
  Can the function or activity be eliminated? In its entirety? Internally with external provision of the same service at less cost?

- Compare and contrast activities
  Which activities are necessary and unnecessary in the providing of the product or service?
  Which activities are performed efficiently and inefficiently?
  Which activities can be eliminated or reduced in scope immediately?
  Which activities can be improved immediately or in the short term?
  Which activities can be compared to other activities as best practices?

(continues)

Exhibit 3.3 *(Continued)*

- Identify for external benchmarking study
Identification of mental models, belief systems, and performance drivers
Selection of operational benchmarks and performance measures
Identification of benchmarking targets: organization, department, function, activities, processes
Identification of type of study: competitive, industry, and/or best in class

WORKING WITH CLOSELY HELD AND FAMILY-OWNED BUSINESSES

When working with large publicly held corporations, management is working with "other people's money" (OPM) and often may be less concerned as to the results of the internal benchmarking study then they are with maintaining its power and control. However, when working with a closely held and/or family owned business, the owners, who are also usually top management, are using money out of their own pockets and are much more interested in results that maximize economy, efficiency, and effectiveness. In such businesses, the owner bosses can be as eccentric (and obnoxious) as they desire since they have ownership. In working with such organizations, the study team may spend as much time dealing with the owners' excesses and family dynamics as they spend with business concerns. The elements of these eccentricities become performance drivers which affect the performance—usually negative—of all employees.

The family business is a business enterprise where two or more family members (e.g., husband and wife, parent and child, brothers and sisters) own and/or manage the business. Such a family business, which is normally privately owned, has many advantages to the family owners, such as the following:

- **Power and control:** family-owners make any decisions they desire.
- **Different strokes:** family-owners may take special privileges.

- **Accountability:** family members enjoy different criteria from hired management and employees.
- **Job security:** typically family members do not get fired.
- **Company policies:** do not apply the same to family members.
- **Flex time:** family members can come and go as they wish (if they come in late, they can leave early).
- **Compensation:** family-owners can pay themselves whatever the business can bear, in salary, benefits, reimbursed "business expenses," and so on.
- **Business write-offs:** family owners can charge whatever they can to the business.
- **Family inheritance:** the family business can be a living trust for the children.
- **Retirement in place:** the family business can provide a place for older family members to draw a salary while in early retirement or semi-retirement.

For members of the internal benchmarking team, the above advantages to the family business owner may become constraints in the conducting of the internal benchmarking study. However, the study team needs to understand these performance drivers and take them into account as they may adversely affect the results of the business and the performance expectations of family members and other employees. In addition, family-owners may balk at the study team's sound business practice recommendations, even when these recommendations are in their best interest. This is especially true when such a recommendation gets in the way of one or more of the above items or others.

The closely held and/or family business may also have some potential drawbacks to the owners, which include the following:

- **Workaholism:** the business becomes the owner's life.
- **Crisis management:** the owner's inability to properly manage and control the business.
- **Lack of business acumen:** the owner's on-the-job training versus the acquisition of professional management skills.

- **Success in spite of yourself:** the owner becoming successful more on the basis of falling into a lucrative business niche and/or hiring exceptional employees.
- **Minimal rewards:** the owners spending long hours at the business with less than desired compensation.
- **Inability to get out of the business:** the owners may have too much of their own resources tied up in the business and they don't know what else to do.
- **Family incompetence:** the owners, spouses, children, or other relatives may be in positions of importance but are incompetent to do the right job.

The internal benchmarking team needs to identify the drawbacks mentioned above as well as many others as to mental models, belief systems, and negative performance drivers which have an adverse effect on operations and results. As management is also the owners of the business, they may be willing to change all of the above or they may decide to leave things the way they are. The internal benchmarking team needs to understand what is changeable and what is not in the conduct of the study and the development of practical and reasonable recommendations as to best practices.

PRIORITIZING CRITICAL AREAS FOR BENCHMARKING

As a result of developing organizational benchmarks, plans, and basic business principles, the company should have identified those critical areas for benchmarking. Which areas to include in the company's initial internal benchmarking study may be apparent. There may be only a few (or just one) major critical areas to consider in the initial study or some areas that are so critical they need immediate attention. If there are a large number of critical areas, it is good practice to prioritize which areas to include in this study, which ones to benchmark in the future, and which items can be substantially improved without benchmarking. For instance, the organization might schedule their critical areas as shown in Exhibit 3.4.

Exhibit 3.4 Schedule of Critical Areas

Critical Area	Cost	Impact	Improvement Potential	Rank	*P/F/I
Manufacturing processes	$3,000,000	High	100	1	P
Purchasing	$ 800,000	Medium	60	5	F
Sales department	$ 600,000	High	50	2	P
Engineering	$ 340,000	Medium	80	6	F
Accounting/ financial	$ 220,000	Medium	60	7	F
Receiving/ shipping	$ 80,000	Low	80	8	I
Customer service	$ 60,000	High	100	3	P
Quality control	$ 55,000	High	80	4	I

*P/F/I = Present Study, Future, and Immediate

The prioritization of which areas to include in the company's internal benchmarking study is usually done by brainstorming with top management, other members of management, operations personnel, members of the internal benchmarking study team, and others such as outside consultants, providers of outsourced services, external accountants, and so on. The criteria to be considered in such prioritization of critical areas should include which areas could be most improved through the identification of best practices, which areas offer the greatest potential for improvement, and which ones impact the customer (stakeholders) most critically. Remember the 80/20 rule: 20% of your activities cause 80% of your problems. Concentrate on the elephants, not the mice. In addition, the company needs to consider such things as resources of time, personnel, and costs. Normally, this helps to determine the number of areas to benchmark at one time, based on the immediacy of each critical area.

A tool to assist the company in identifying its critical areas for improvement is an organization-wide initial survey form, as shown in Exhibit 3.5.

Exhibit 3.5   Organization-Wide Initial Survey Form

PLANNING AND BUDGETING

1. How does the organization plan? Describe the system of planning.
2. Does a strategic and/or long-range plan exist? Attach copy.
3. Do current plans exist? Attach copy.
4. What are plans for expansion or improvement?
5. What are plans for physical plant development?
6. What are plans for future financing?
7. What are personnel plans?
8. How does the organization budget? Describe the budgeting system.
9. Does a current budget exist? Obtain or prepare copy.
10. Do budget versus actual statistics exist for the last five years? Obtain or prepare copy.

PERSONNEL AND STAFFING

1. Does an organization chart exist? Obtain or prepare copy.
2. Do functional job descriptions exist for each block on the organization chart? Obtain or prepare copy.
3. Do staffing statistics by functional area exist? Obtain or prepare copy.
4. Is there a system of employee evaluations? Obtain or prepare copy.
5. How are employees recruited, hired, evaluated, and fired? Describe procedures.
6. What are promotional policies? Describe.
7. How are new employees oriented? Describe.
8. How are raises and promotions determined? Describe.
9. Is there a grievance mechanism? Describe.
10. What type of personnel records are maintained? Obtain copies.

Exhibit 3.5 *(Continued)*

MANAGEMENT

1. Does a Board of Directors exist? Attach list of names and credentials.
2. Who is considered top management? Attach list of names and credentials.
3. Who is considered middle management? Attach list of names and credentials.
4. Who is considered lower management? Attach list of names and credentials.
5. How adequate are existing reports in furnishing information for making management's decisions? Describe.
6. Are there internal downward communication tools to the staff? Attach copies.
7. How many levels of management are there? Describe.
8. What is the ratio of management to operations personnel? Provide data.

POLICIES AND PROCEDURES

1. Who is responsible for setting company policies?
2. Do written policies exist? Obtain copy.
3. Are written policies current?
4. Who is responsible for establishing systems and procedures?
5. Are systems and procedures documented? Obtain or prepare copy.
6. Are systems and procedures current?

ACCOUNTING SYSTEM

1. What is the chart of accounts that is used? Obtain or prepare copy.
2. Is the accounting system mechanized? Obtain documentation.
3. What financial reports are produced? Obtain copies.
4. Is there an internal audit function? By whom and to whom?
5. Are there internal operating reports produced? Obtain copies and determine uses.
6. Is a cost accounting system used? Describe or obtain documentation.

(continues)

Exhibit 3.5   *(Continued)*

REVENUES

1. What are the sources of revenue for the last five years? Obtain or prepare statistics.
2. Have there been any substantial changes during this period? Document them.
3. Are actual versus budgeted data available? Obtain or prepare copy.
4. Is there a reporting system for revenues? Describe or obtain documentation.
5. Are revenues reported by product line, product, customer? Describe.

EXPENSES

1. What are the major expense accounts used? Obtain or prepare copy.
2. What are actual expenses for these accounts for the last five years? Obtain copy.
3. Have there been any substantial changes during this period? Document them.
4. Are actual versus budgeted data available? Obtain or prepare copy.
5. Does a cost accounting system exist for expenses? Describe.
6. Are any sophisticated systems used, such as flexible budgeting or activity-based costing? Describe.

COMPUTERIZED PROCEDURES

1. Where are computer systems presently located in the organization? Obtain or prepare copy of locations and personnel.
2. What computer equipment is used? Obtain or prepare copy of equipment with capabilities.
3. What is total cost of equipment rental or purchase price if owned?
4. What are the major applications computerized? Obtain or prepare copy of list of applications, with application documentation.
5. What types of processing are available? Batch, on-line, real time, networked, microcomputers, minicomputers, main frames, etc.

Exhibit 3.5 *(Continued)*

PURCHASING

1. What is purchasing authority? Obtain or prepare copy of policy relative to purchasing authority.
2. Is purchasing centralized or decentralized? Describe operations.
3. How are purchase requisitions initiated? Describe general procedures.
4. Who determines quality and quantity desired? Describe procedures.
5. Are purchase orders used? Describe procedures.
6. Are competitive bidding procedures used? Describe procedures.

PRODUCTION CONTROL

1. Is a manufacturing control system used? Is it computerized? Obtain or prepare copy of general procedures.
2. What types of manufacturing processes are used? Describe.
3. What is location(s) of manufacturing facilities? Document.
4. Are production cost centers used to control the routing of manufacturing orders? Obtain or prepare copy of cost centers.
5. Is a manufacturing cost system used? Obtain or prepare copy of cost accounting procedures.
6. Are operational and management reports provided to control manufacturing operations? Obtain copies.

INVENTORY CONTROL

1. Is an inventory control system used? Is it computerized? Obtain or prepare copy of general procedures.
2. What type of inventory control procedures are used? Describe.
3. Where are inventory storeroom locations? Obtain or prepare copy of locations and describe storeroom procedures.
4. How are inventory records maintained? Describe procedures.
5. Is perpetual inventory maintained? Describe procedures.
6. Are inventory statistics and data maintained? Obtain data as to items in inventory, dollar value, usage, on-hand balances, and so on.
7. What is basis for reordering inventory items and how are reorder quantities determined? Describe procedures.

OPERATIONAL REVIEW

Once the company's critical areas are identified for inclusion in the internal benchmark study, an initial operational review should provide data on the operation of related activities such as:

- **Who is involved and how they relate to the activity, its desired results, and each other.** Data to be considered could include the number of individuals, relative positions, method of organization and management, and so on.
- **Why each individual is involved and his or her value or non–value-added activities.** The reviewer could look at such things as to whether these individuals perform necessary operations, spend too much non-value-added time, have any special expertise, or bear responsibility—or whether there are unnecessary activities and personnel and excess organizational structure.
- **Which activities are done.** Which needs to be done, can be done more efficiently, or is being done well (a best practice)?
- **Why each activity is done.** Does each of the activities relate to desired goals and objectives of the organization, and is each one performed most effectively.
- **What resources are allocated to each activity.** Is the allocation most economical, are resources excessive, or are they deficient to achieve desired results.

The focus of the operational review is to provide understanding and clearly document existing practices and procedures by:

- Identification of key aspects of the company, department, or work unit's activities and performance results
- Identification of mental models and belief systems as well as inherent, structural, and performance drivers
- Identification of critical operational areas and opportunities for improvement (one part learning from another)

- Establishment of channels of communication within the company, from top management down to the operations level, from operations to management, and across functional lines
- Identification of desirable practices (best practices and areas of excellence) that can be improved as well as replicated in other areas of the company
- Establishment of standards for good practices to reflect the adoption of best practices

Defining the elements of each activity; determining whether the activity is value or non–value-added, and what each individual does in the process and why is the basis for analysis which will lead to positive improvements.

INTERNAL BENCHMARKING COMPARISONS

In performing the internal benchmarking study, there are a number of bases on present practices may be compared, such as the following:

- Comparisons between individuals performing similar functions within the same work unit
- Comparative analysis between different work units within the company which perform similar functions
- Comparisons to industry standards
- Comparisons to published benchmark standards
- Comparisons to tests of reasonableness

In analyzing present conditions, the members of the internal benchmarking study team must be aware of which conditions will meet organizational goals and objectives.

In determining the proper benchmark for comparison to a specific activity, the study team could review such areas as relevant legislation, existing contracts, policy statements, systems and procedures, internal and external regulations, responsibility and authority relationships, standards, schedules, plans and budgets, principles of good management and administration, and so on. In determining the correct benchmark for a specific function, the study team should answer the following questions for the activity:

- What should it be?
- What do you measure against?
- What is the standard procedure or practice?
- Is it a formal procedure or an informal practice?

This results in comparing what is to what should be—the benchmark.

In evaluating operating practices, the study team should be aware that procedures are formal methods of doing things, usually documented in writing and prescribed by management. Practices are the actual way that work activities are performed and are rarely documented in written form.

INTERNAL BENCHMARKS

Some examples of internal benchmarks for such comparison purposes include benchmarks which are internal to the organization:

- Organizational policy statements
- Legislation, laws, and regulations
- Contractual arrangements
- Funding arrangements
- Organizational and departmental plans: goals and objectives
- Budgets, schedules, and detail plans

Some benchmarks are developed by the internal benchmarking team:

- Internal performance statistics: by individual or work unit
- Performance of similar organizations
- Industry or functionally related statistics
- Past and present performance

- Engineered standards
- Special analysis or studies
- Benchmarking team's judgment
- Sound business practices
- Good common business sense

Sometimes it is difficult to determine exactly what the benchmark should be. Internal management may see it as one thing, while the internal benchmarking team may see it as another. For example, management may see the benchmark as always having inventory on hand for customer shipment, while the study team may see the benchmark for inventory as getting out of the inventory business and producing to customer orders and required delivery dates. The following example depicts a situation where this conflict of agreed benchmarks exists.

The AAA Sales Company was in the consumer product distribution business, selling their line of manufactured products to wholesalers and brokers. The internal benchmarking team was working with the company to develop effective inventory control and sales statistics systems. The goal of the study for the benchmarking team was to identify and implement best practices so that the company could manufacture their products based on customer requirements and desired delivery dates to minimize inventory levels (with zero inventory as a goal). The company also wanted to develop a reporting system which allowed them to determine which products were selling and which sales (products and customers) were making the best profits.

The internal benchmarking team identified and implemented effective best practice systems to minimize the amount of inventory on hand. The study team had established a system whereby inventory data were integrated with customer sales data, ordering and receipt patterns, and delivery requirements so that product could be shipped directly to customers as finished. AAA management prided themselves on the ability to deliver product to customers on time when needed. To accomplish this, management established the policy that inventory stock-outs were not to be tolerated. This corporate belief system of no inventory stock-outs was contrary to the benchmarking team's best practice of allowing for just-in-time vendor deliveries and just-in-time customer shipments from manufacturing.

As a result of the old corporate belief system, inventory levels had swollen greatly, even with the new system, for many of the company's historically fast moving items. At the same time, customers were experiencing a downtrend in overall consumer spending resulting in fewer orders to AAA. The result was a large stockpile of finished goods inventory. The cause of this condition was management's inability to change its thinking to not be in the inventory business. The symptom was too much inventory. Management's solution was to offer sales incentives for these items as a means of reducing inventory levels.

A few customers responded to AAA's incentives, so management decided to increase the sales incentives. Eventually, AAA management reduced the sales amount to a number where deals were made with a number of customers, even where profits were negative. AAA management got rid of their excess inventory. However, conditions soon changed and these items were in demand again. AAA's major customers had sufficient quantities on hand at those lower prices, while AAA couldn't sell the inventory of these items at any price. AAA management's solution had created the cause of their net problem.

COMPARISONS BETWEEN INDIVIDUALS

Comparing individuals performing similar functions (e.g., production workers, engineers, salespeople, accounting personnel, and so on) is not an exact science, as each individual's function may be slightly different. However, better practices can be identified to use one's expertise and ways of doing the job with others. Such automatic transference of how one performs an activity well to another who does not perform the activity as well is usually not accomplished easily. There is usually some reluctance on the part of the individual who does the job well to share his or her expertise with those who do not perform the job as well. For example, the following example discusses some of the difficulties in comparing the work results of individuals performing similar functions and the ability to transfer good work habits and results from one to another.

We were part of an internal benchmarking team working with a small manufacturer of specialty boxes. At one time, this specialty box business was quite profitable with profit margins of 43 percent. Now, however, competition and the competitors' use of new, less costly methods have reduced profit margins of the company to under 20 percent and falling. Still not too shabby, but cause for alarm before profit margins sink below zero.

The owners of the company asked us to benchmark their internal productivity relative to similar functions, individuals performing the same activities, and their competition—in both manufacturing as well as the office areas. The company had increased sales to a level that top management believed was practical for their capabilities and had cut costs to the extent they believed was realistic without harming operations drastically. Now, they believed they had to increase productivity in all areas to reduce unit costs, negotiate sales prices more competitively, and increase resultant profits.

We reviewed manufacturing operations and found that all of the company's processes had been automated to the practical extent possible. Those functions still requiring personal intervention were of a mechanical and measurable nature (e.g., storeroom operations, loading automated equipment, movement from one process to another, folding, packing, shipping, and so on). The company had a fairly well-designed reporting system over these operations which told plant management productivity by employee and compared such results to other similar employees and an expected standard.

The foreperson in each area was to analyze such reports the following morning and to take remedial action. Such action typically consisted of berating those employees who compared poorly to others and/or the standard. We noted minimal improvement (in fact just the opposite) from this management practice. We analyzed each employee's performance over a period of time (number of good items produced and number of rejects, rework, and returned items) which resulted in a pattern for each employee, a narrow range of productivity for each employee and all employees working in a similar function—in other words each employee and function had his or her own standard or level of production.

Interestingly, as each employee's productivity increased (no doubt after a talking-to by the foreperson), the number of rejects increased. We concluded that each employee and function had developed his or her own narrow range of productivity within quality expectations—and present reporting and management practices weren't creating any positive improvements. Payroll analysis disclosed minimal differences between hourly rates. In fact, compensation was based on seniority (number of years with the company), regardless of the level of quality productivity. Production employees had no real incentive to improve productivity, only to survive.

We analyzed employee productivity based on seniority and related hourly rates. There would seem to be a direct relationship between seniority, compensation, and productivity. The longer an employee had been on the job and the more they were compensated, there was an expectation that productivity increased as well. Theoretically, one would expect increased productivity for increased compensation, the additional productivity more than making up for the increased cost of labor. However, our analysis disclosed that the number of good units produced per dollar of payroll cost increased inversely to the number of years employed and the related amount of compensation. In other words, the newer, less costly employees were more productive per dollar of wages than the older employees.

Our review of the office functions disclosed that there were no productivity expectations, no controls or reporting over results, and no effective means of evaluation. Employee evaluation as to which employee was doing the better job was at the sole subjective appraisal of the employee's manager. In analyzing specific office function areas (e.g., purchasing, customer service, personnel, engineering, accounting, data processing, and so on), we found them all overstaffed, related to results achieved. It was questionable if many of the office activities were really needed—in whole or in part. There was no way to determine results being produced, relative productivity, and the cost to the company. Our analysis also disclosed that the younger and/or newer hires were doing the bulk of the work while the older, "more experienced," higher-paid employees were doing the least they could get away with. Most of their time was spent talking to each other and watching the newer employees work.

It was apparent that present procedures weren't working. There was no real incentive for increasing productivity in either the plant or the office—actually just the opposite. Compensation was based more on time put in with the company rather than what was put into the time. We believed that a system needed to be implemented which would better correlate productivity with compensation. The first step was to install procedures to ensure that each employee knew exactly what was expected of him or her and the results to be achieved. The next step was to determine the present competencies of each employee and the related levels of quality productivity. You can't make a .300 hitter out of a .225 hitter just because you want to—you have to start with each employee.

We then developed a method of compensation which rewarded each employee based on results achieved, which would be seen as equitable to all employees. To make our point to management, we used three employees with differing levels of present productivity and compensation which were as follows:

- Employee A   8 units per hour $12/hour

- Employee B   10 units per hour $10/hour

- Employee C   12 units per hour $ 8/hour

We asked management, based solely on the levels of productivity, to rank these employees according to seniority with the company. Management placed them in C, B, A order. When we told them the order in reality was just the opposite, they wouldn't believe us until we disclosed the actual data. They all nodded and said in unison "that must be the plant, we know we have trouble there." When we told them that these weren't plant personnel but customer service employees, and that the plant numbers were even worse, they became silent. Finally the Chief Financial Officer (CFO) asked what could be done about this. We recommended that the company institute a three-step plan of expectations, competencies, and compensation.

We developed quality expectations and results for each function in the company and established related compensations based on the level of productivity achieved (e.g., 8 units = $8/hour, 10 units = $10/hour, 12 units = $12/hour). Each employee was compensated based on results, not on seniority. If the company wanted to give additional compensation for years in, so be it, but separate from results for compensation.

We looked at each employee's competencies and determine how to make each more productive and better compensated. We agreed that the lowest present level of productivity in each function was acceptable—but only for a related level of compensation. If the employee wanted to earn additional compensation, he or she would have to increase their productivity. We knew they wouldn't be able to do this on their own or under the present system of control, reporting, and management. We replaced 12 forepeople and six supervisors/managers with four coaches, whose job was to help each employee continually improve.

As each employee improved and productivity increased, each one was compensated at the higher level of productivity. As overall profits increased and management calculated the results of increased productivity, additional compensation was shared with the employees. With this system, we accomplished a number of positive improvements which included:

- Making each employee an entrepreneur (in business for him or herself) responsible for their own level of compensation
- Fostering cooperation (and eliminating competition) among employees as it is now to all of their benefits to increase productivity and resultant profits
- Creating an atmosphere of self-disciplined behavior characterized by individual responsibility, working together, and self-learning

- Eliminating too many so-called foreperson and management personnel with the use of fewer coaches to create a program of continuous improvement and productivity, rather than stagnation and unnecessary costs
- Eliminating costly compensation practices with an inverse relationship to results achieved
- Reducing the number of personnel as levels of staff are related to productivity levels in direct operating areas as well as management
- Using older experienced personnel (where productivity levels can no longer be maintained) as coaches and facilitators so that their experience can be used effectively on a more cost-effective basis
- Creating effective systems and procedures which allow for the identification and implementation of ongoing best practices in a program of continuous improvements
- Identification and elimination of non-helpful systems such as a military model of organizational structure set up for management policing and control of employees, compensation systems which reward seniority rather than results, budget systems which constrain operations rather then support operations, and so on.

The concept is to develop a best practice that provides for meeting the goals and objectives of the benchmark—in this case, to increase productivity at the least cost. Once the best practice is successfully implemented, it is then subject to continual review for ongoing enhancements and improvements. In such a learning organization, all functions and activities are subject to continual review and change.

ALTERNATIVE CRITERIA

In some instances, company management may not be able to identify appropriate organizational, departmental, or functional internal benchmarks. In these instances, internal benchmarks must be developed to compare to present operations. In the absence of existing internal standards or benchmarking criteria with which to evaluate performance, there are other alternative approaches, including comparative analysis, the use of borrowed statistics, the test of reasonableness, and performance measure analysis.

Comparative Analysis

Comparative analysis is the technique that, where specific internal standards do not exist for comparison, can compare the reviewed activities to similar situations within the company. This analysis can be accomplished in a number of ways, which include the following:

- Current performance can be compared to past performance, for the entire department, for a specific function or activity, or for specific employees.
- One work unit's performance can be compared with another similar work unit's within the organization.
- Performance can be compared between workers within the same work unit or other similar operations within the company.

Comparing current to past periods has the advantage of disclosing trends in performance. For example, if the cost per employee procedures manual rises from year to year, you might question whether prices have risen, if inefficiencies in manual preparation have increased, if employees are being given larger quantities, or whether a better quality of material is used. You can then analyze the situation further to determine exactly why the cost per procedures manual has increased. In this example, the criteria by which actual performance is evaluated is not a predetermined plan or a formal set of performance standards; simply what was done in prior years. Using such comparisons does not provide sufficient data to tell whether the rise in procedures manual prices per employee is good or bad, or whether costs are too high. This method does, however, identify the causes so that management can judge performance as it occurred. Although it is possible to note and examine trends by this method, meaningful comparisons of alternative methods or procedures require a different approach.

The comparison of two different but similar work units normally provides the opportunity to evaluate different approaches to operations management. By determining the results of different operational approaches, the benchmarking team can make some helpful recommendations for improving efficiency and effectiveness.

There are, however, some disadvantages in comparing two separate but similar work units. The major disadvantage is the failure to recognize factors which justify differences between the two units. For example, it is difficult to compare manufacturing locations, as no two facilities may have exactly the same type of manufacturing systems, hire the same type of employees, use the same type of equipment, or have the same proximity to materials and other essentials.

Each manufacturing location would, however, have many of the same types of problems regardless of their differences. The similarity of problems allows the benchmarking team to analyze how each location's management group handles these common problems. The team can then analyze such alternatives for improving the efficiency and effectiveness of operations and resultant recommendations can reflect the team's judgment based on the results each alternative produces.

Comparisons between workers within the same work unit or different but similar work units within the company provide the perspective of how different workers perform the same activities. Such perspective can help the benchmarking study team to determine a best practice by a specific worker or workers which can become the short-term benchmarking standard for the other workers. However, there should be some caution in implementing or dictating such a standard as many times what one (or more) worker can do is not always automatically transferable to other workers. There needs to be an effective plan for gradual transferability. However, what is important is that such comparisons disclose the possibility of better practices or increased productivity.

The comparison of an individual worker's productivity over a period of time may also be useful in disclosing positive or negative changes in the worker's performance. Such trends may help to identify positive changes or practices in performing the same activities which others could use, or in identifying negative changes which can be corrected or eliminated.

The Use of Borrowed Statistics: Industry and Published Benchmarks

Many groups and organizations throughout the country, such as manufacturers, hospitals, banking associations, and so on, provide uniform and comparable industry and benchmark standards for evaluating performance.

In addition, many professional associations and journals publish benchmarking results and standards on an ongoing or periodic basis. These borrowed standards can then be used to compare performances of organizations in similar endeavors. Although such comparisons would make performance evaluation quicker and easier, there are some disadvantages to this procedure as well.

One disadvantage in this method of comparison is that national averages and broad-based statistics hardly ever relate to specific situations. Thus, while such statistics provide some indications of the organization's performance, they can not be used for precise measurement or evaluation. Another disadvantage is that very few national averages or uniform statistics actually exist. In those cases where such statistics do exist, such as by standard industry code, hospitals, banks, service industries, schools, libraries, and so on, either they relate to only a small portion of the areas subject to internal benchmarking, or they are limited to very restricted areas, and are of minimal use.

The Test of Reasonableness

When there are no identifiable internal standards, and comparisons with other organizations are difficult, or borrowed benchmarks are unavailable, the internal benchmarking team can still test organizational performance compared to a benchmark based on the test of reasonableness. Through experience, members of the internal benchmarking team (including outside consultants and others) become familiar with how things are done economically, efficiently, and effectively in other organizations. The team members should then be able to relate these experiences to the current functions included in the present internal benchmarking study.

Accordingly, the internal benchmarking team can often spot operational irregularities and weaknesses that might escape the notice of others without such a background. In internal benchmarking, perceptions of a situation are based on the eyes of the beholder—in this case the cumulative experience of the internal benchmarking team. In addition, there exists what may be termed "general standards of proper work practices" that apply to good management in any field, public or private. For example, work done in a loose, unsatisfactory, and inefficient manner often can be identified even without specific standards or benchmarks. Often this work has been acceptable—"that's the way we've always done it." Or, the methods of the organization or work unit may be so ingrained, the workers never question their procedures or fail to accept them as good practices. Observers who are not connected to the activity can often see such deficiencies quickly as they have no preconceived ideas in their minds as to what should be.

Obsolete inventory, excessive supplies, personnel continually absent from work, abuse in resource use such as automobiles and expense accounts, negligence in processing documents or handling cash funds are all examples of items which the test of reasonableness can evaluate. The test of reasonableness can also be used as a tool to quickly review operating areas not subjected to detailed analysis. Even where the study team has analyzed in detail, its conclusions can still be examined for reasonableness. This ensures that the team has not become so engrossed in statistics or its own preconceived belief systems that its members overlook important items or place too much weight on minor ones. The test of reasonableness can also serve as the application of good common sense or prudent business practice to the situation. Many of these items listed above can be identified through direct observation, others through simple data collection.

Examples of items which can be evaluated through the test of reasonableness are shown in Exhibit 3.6.

Performance Measure Analysis

A business organization periodically produces financial reports which typically include a balance sheet, income statement, and sometimes a statement of cash flows. While these financial statements provide certain data to management as to how well the company has

Exhibit 3.6 Items to Consider for the Test of Reasonableness

Obsolete inventory

Excessive materials and supplies

Non-conducive work environment

Uneven distribution of workload

Sloppy work practices

Personnel who are continually absent from work

Abuse in the use of resources such as automobiles and expense accounts

Negligence in processing documents

Improper handling of cash funds

Poor or non-responsive customer service

Unhelpful systems such as ineffective planning and budget procedures

Poor work flow or work layout

Unwieldy organizational hierarchies

Non-integration of functions

Poor communication systems

Unidentified performance drivers and measures

Inadequate reporting and control systems

Improper use of computer systems

Over or under facility capacity

performed financially (from a generally accepted accounting principle basis) for the preceding period, there is additional operational data required to assess whether the company's progress satisfactory. Often management will define these measures as guidelines for operations personnel to meet or surpass. These measures are known by various names such as key operating indicators, major operating statistics, and performance measures. If such performance measures have been identified, the study team can appraise the quality of such measures (and whether they are the right measures) and evaluate actual results against the measures. If performance measures have not yet been established, then the study team can identify these measures and then evaluate actual operations against them. In either case, such analysis can provide the study team with information as to the identification of critical areas, benchmark performance gaps, areas for immediate improvement, areas for internal or external benchmarking, best practices, and so on.

Performance measures can be established for the organization as a whole such as number of new hires, on time reporting, quality criteria (e.g., zero rework), cost containment (e.g., no budget increases based on activity levels), and so on. Performance measures can also be established for each department, function, or activity of the company such as the sales department—in total or by sales person:

- Amount of sales in dollars—by customer, product line, and product
- Number of sales contacts—by existing and potential customers
- Profit margin per sale
- Dollar amount of average sale
- Actual customer sales compared to sales forecast
- Amount of time spent on customer service—by customer
- Number and amount of orders received unsolicited

Or the manufacturing department:

- Number of production orders entered into production on time
- Number of orders completed on time
- Amount of scrap, rework, or rejects
- Number of orders in production that agree with the production schedule
- Number of orders shipped to the customer (in full) on time
- Amount of backlog, orders not on schedule, orders completed on a partial basis
- Cost variances: material, labor, assigned activities

It is important that the internal benchmarking team clearly understand the internal benchmark or performance measure it is evaluating. Often, management and operations personnel may focus on a specific measure for evaluation and improvement. They will put a great deal of effort into measuring and improving the measure. However, the measure may be the wrong one for the function involved. For example, the manufacturing operations department may believe that one of the measures of efficiency is to maximize the amount of scrap produced from manufacturing so that it can maximize the amount of money to be realized from the sale of scrap. Having such a measure will obscure the real benchmark for manufacturing, which is not to have the scrap in the first place. Having the measure as it is places the emphasis on the collection and resale of scrap rather than the elimination of scrap.

Here's another example of how misunderstood internal benchmarks result in the wrong performance measure and results. Jim Pierce has been the Manager of Customer Relations of a major consumer goods manufacturer for the last twelve years. No one remembers exactly how he became manager, except that most of the employees had quit the department at the time of his promotion due to the overbearing nature of the previous manager. Jim had stuck it out and stayed, and since he had seniority over the other two remaining employees, his loyalty was rewarded with a promotion to manager when the previous manager left the company.

Jim was a rather unassuming person, and this trait carried over to his managing. He left those employees who reported to him fairly well alone. His philosophy of managing (his personal belief system) was just for each employee to do his or her job and not get him into trouble with higher management. If an employee was any bit of a problem, Jim would help that employee get transferred to another department within the company, often with a promotion to a higher position. In this way, none of his employees ever threatened to take over his job. As a result, higher management received very few complaints about Jim or his department—from either employees or customers.

The internal benchmarking team was conducting a review of the entire organization, which included the Customer Relations Department. At that time, there were fourteen full-time employees in the Customer Relations Department, plus Jim and a secretary. Through a review of operations, which included personal interviews with all employees, the study team determined that the department mission was to clear all customer complaints and concerns at whatever cost within one busy day. For instance, employees would grant customer credit and ship additional merchandise with no investigation of the situation. Although, in some instances this may have been the correct remedy, in most instances this was not found to be the case. In effect, Jim was not effectively managing the department for the right results. He was managing the employees to mechanically process customer complaints rather than to determine the causes of the complaints so that the company could eliminate such causes and future similar complaints. If the Customer Relations Department was doing the right job, customer complaints would continually reduce, as would the size of the department. If absolutely successful, the company would have no need for employees to handle customer complaints.

INDICATORS OF INTERNAL BENCHMARKING DEFICIENCIES

There are numerous indicators of operating deficiencies that the internal benchmarking team may consider in its internal benchmarking review. Some of these indicators relate to general organizational and departmental principles of good management and operations, while others relate to less than best practices for specific functions or activities. Some of these indicators include:

Management and Organization

- Poor planning and decision-making
- Too broad a span of control
- Badly designed systems and procedures
- Excessive crisis management
- Poor channels of communication
- Inadequate delegation of authority
- Excessive organizational changes
- Unwieldy organizational structure
- Non-value-added management and operations personnel

Personnel Relations

- Inadequate hiring, orientation, training, evaluation, and promotion procedures
- Lack of clearly communicated job expectations
- Idle, excessive, or not enough personnel
- Poor employee morale
- Excessive overtime and/or absenteeism
- Unclear responsibility and authority relationships

Manufacturing Operations

- Poor manufacturing methods
- Inefficient plant layout
- Excessive rework, scrap, or salvage
- Idle equipment and/or operations personnel
- Insufficient or excessive equipment
- Excessive production or operating costs
- Lack of effective production scheduling procedures
- Poor housekeeping
- Excessive, slow moving, or obsolete inventory

Purchasing

- Not achieving best prices, timeliness, and quality from vendors
- Favoritism to certain vendors
- Lack of effective competitive bidding procedures
- Not using most effective systems such as blanket purchase orders, traveling requisitions, telephone ordering, electronic data transfer, and so on
- Excessive emergency purchase
- Lack of a value analysis program to look continually for purchasing economies and efficiencies
- Purchasing unnecessarily expensive items
- Unmet procurement schedules
- Excessive returns to vendors

Financial Indicators

- Poor profit/loss ratios
- Poor return on investment
- Unfavorable cost or operating ratios
- Unfavorable or unexplained cost or budget variances
- Increasing cost trends or decreasing profit trends
- Inadequate or decreasing cash flow
- Decrease in profitability: organization-wide, product line, product, customer

Complaints

- Customers: bad products or poor service
- Employees: grievances, gripes, or negative exit interview comments
- Vendors: poor quality or untimely deliveries
- Production: unmet schedules, unavailable material, late deliveries, poor quality, excessive rework, scrap, or rejects, and so on

81

INTERNAL BENCHMARKING OPERATIONAL REVIEW TOOLS

Once the internal benchmarking team is clear as to the organizational, departmental, and functional benchmarks for the critical areas included in the study, the next step is to review the related operations in detail. The purpose of the operational review is to compare present practices to what they should be as the benchmark, and determine the best procedures for closing and surpassing the benchmark gap. There are various tools which can be used to conduct such an internal benchmarking operational review. These tools include:

- Operational survey forms
- Organization charts and functional job descriptions
- Systems or process flowcharts
- Layout flow diagrams

These tools and their effective use provide objective analysis of existing systems, procedures, and practices leading toward the identification of areas for positive change such as excessive levels of non-value added work being done. Typically, the internal benchmarking operational review leads to immediate operational improvements as the company reduces or eliminates unnecessary job functions, work steps, or cumbersome work flows. In addition, the organization gains more in-depth knowledge about its current operating systems and procedures, allowing it to identify and eliminate non-value-added activities. Implementing less costly, more efficient, and more effective procedures provides immediate operating improvements, more efficient allocation of resources, increased customer service, and more effective positive cash conversion.

As a result of the internal benchmarking operational review, identification of good and bad aspects of existing practices, personnel requirements, performance drivers, and external benchmarking targets will be made. This will allow for involved personnel to immediately implement identified improvements while the external benchmarking process gets under way. The goal of the internal benchmarking operational review is to bring present operations up to best practices within the internal knowledge of the organization. At this point, further internal improvements should be the responsibility of operations personnel for each function and activity in a program of continuous improvements. As part of conducting the internal benchmarking operational review, the study team should work closely with operations personnel so that operations personnel are properly trained to assume the responsibilities for continual change subsequent to the conclusion of the study. Often, particularly for smaller organizations, an effective internal benchmarking study may exclude the need for a lengthy and costly external benchmarking study.

Operational Survey Forms

We hear a lot about a company's corporate culture—especially a number of years ago when this was a buzz word. Although the internal benchmarking team can probably describe a company's prevalent behavior or image or working atmosphere, it is fairly difficult to capture what we call corporate culture. It is generally a composite of all of the company's mental models, belief systems, and performance drivers. Many times an organization works extremely hard to develop a prevalent image for its employees and public, only to find it is making a somewhat different impression. In most cases, corporate reality is much different than the presumed corporate culture. It is very difficult for an organization to change to its corporate culture. The internal benchmarking study is a tool to assist the company to do this.

For instance, the Apex Telephone Company provided telephone services to a three state area. At one time they were a virtual monopoly, regulated but the only game in town. If a resident wanted telephone service, he or she had to go to Apex. Apex was quite arrogant about providing telephone service. They would come out for telephone installations and repairs when they were ready, and if a customer did not pay their bill they would turn off the service immediately. Their corporate culture was one of a public louse. As things happen sometimes to support the contention that there is a system of justice, the court system agreed with a competitor and decreed that other telephone companies could provide the same telephone services. Customers left Apex in droves to join up with their competitors, who turned out to be nice guys. Apex is now trying to make a complete turnaround, mainly through advertising the fact that they are your old friends. However, those customers who have been coerced back to Apex with promises of change, have found them to be exactly the same. Now, Apex thanks the customer after screwing them.

An organization-wide initial survey form was presented in Exhibit 3.5. This type of survey form is usually found in the front end of the operational review to identify areas of concern within the overall organization. When the internal benchmarking team starts to review and analyze individual departments, functions, or activities, they may also want to use a specific operational survey form for that area. Such survey forms are designed for the specific area under review. The purpose of the operational survey form is to quickly reach those areas responsible for the greatest problems or where there is the largest benchmarking gap between present procedures and best practices.

An example of such an operational survey form for the purchasing function is shown in Exhibit 3.7.

Exhibit 3.7   Purchasing Department: Sample Operational Survey Form

I. Purchasing Department Organizational Status

A. To whom does the head of the Purchasing Department report?

B. What control is exercised over purchasing policy through:

1. Company management outside of purchasing organizational lines of authority?

2. Administrative or other committees?

3. Board of directors?

Exhibit 3.7 *(Continued)*

C. Does a purchasing department organization chart exist? Obtain or prepare copy.

D. What are the duties and responsibilities of each employee in the Purchasing Department? Document by employee.

E. Is there a division of purchasing responsibility among buyers? Document such responsibilities.

II. Purchasing Department Responsibility

A. Is the responsibility of the Purchasing Department clearly defined and understood by:

1. Purchasing department employees?

2. Other department personnel?

B. Does the Purchasing Department have knowledge of conflicting purchasing responsibility assumed by other departments? Document any conflicting responsibilities.

C. Is company policy on purchasing covered by a written manual? Obtain or prepare copy of policy relative to purchasing authority.

D. Are there purchasing activities for which the Purchasing Department has no responsibility or limited responsibility? Document these areas.

E. Do other departments have any relations with vendors? Is there a policy regarding such vendor relations? Document any such relations.

F. Does the Purchasing Department work with operating departments on such matters as:

1. Favorable purchasing opportunities

2. Economic ordering quantities

3. Purchase specification changes

III. Purchasing Authorization

A. What is the general policy for approval of purchases by departments requiring materials? Obtain copy or document policy.

B. Are approval limits covered in written instructions? Obtain copy.

C. Are approval limits definite as to amount and classification of expenditures? Obtain or prepare copy.

(continues)

Exhibit 3.7   *(Continued)*

D. What are policies regarding special approvals for the following? Obtain or prepare copy of policies.

　1. Capital expenditures

　2. Budget limitations prior to purchase commitment

E. What is the approval policy where the final cost of an order exceeds the amount originally estimated on the purchase order?

　1. If the limit of approval of original signer is not exceeded by final cost?

　2. If the limit of approval of original signer is exceeded by final cost?

IV. Physical Facilities

A. Are the layout and general facilities of the Purchasing Department conducive to effective operations? Obtain or prepare copy of physical layout.

B. Are purchasing functions for the following physically set up as appropriate?

　1. Buyers

　2. Expediters

　3. Purchasing specifications unit

　4. Reception area

　5. Salespeople interviews

　6. Purchase order preparation

　7. Support functions

V. Decentralized Purchasing

A. Is there a policy on purchases made by decentralized operating units, such as petty cash funds, sales offices, and so on?

　1. Limits of authority

　2. Reporting responsibility

　3. Review or control by central Purchasing Department

B. Do any operating units have authority to purchase items without the authority of the Purchasing Department? Document.

Exhibit 3.7   *(Continued)*

VI. Purchasing Department Procedures

A. Are Purchasing Department procedures oral or written? Obtain or prepare copy if written.

B. What are procedures regarding:

1. Handling of purchase requisitions

2. Placing of purchase orders

3. Flow of forms

Obtain copy or document.

C. Are there procedures related to vendor bidding? Document.

D. What specialized forms does the Purchasing Department use? Obtain copies of each form. These should be reviewed so that the purpose and usage are thoroughly understood.

E. Are there policies and procedures relative to:

1. Purchasing locally where possible

2. Purchasing from users of company products

F. Does the Purchasing Department maintain or participate in a value analysis program?

Note: In a value analysis program, the Purchasing Department will work with vendors and with affected company departments (such as engineering and manufacturing) in the analysis of specifications, consumption, and requirements. Through such analysis and cooperative effort, it is possible to make savings through redesign, change in specifications, purchase in more economical quantities, or manufacture by the company itself.

Organizational Chart Review

Why do organizations in the private and public sectors organize to conduct their operations? The answer, in most instances, is that is how it is supposed to be. If you didn't have people reporting to other people, those reporting wouldn't know what to do. How could you trust them to do their jobs without someone else responsible to watch them? The traditional organizational hierarchy has become the accepted manner by which to departmentalize people, without the necessity of maintaining individual accountability. When there is trouble within the organization, this hierarchy makes it simple to get rid of the entire department or the departmental scapegoat or troublemaker and avoid facing the real cause of the problem—which may be management policing, control, and the inability to release authority to employees. Often, the cause can be ineffective top and/or middle management, but it is easier to blame the employees than admit to that.

The real answer to why companies organize is so they can accomplish their desired results or benchmarks. In other words, to be most effective (maximize results) in the most economical manner (optimum use of limited resources), using the most efficient methods of operations (best practices). This is known as the three Es of operations—economy, efficiency, and effectiveness. The organizational structure is the tool that is supposed to enable the organization to conduct their business in the desired manner, using limited resources to accomplish maximum results, using best practices of operations. The internal benchmarking team needs to question this principle when they analyze the company's organizational structure. Managers and other employees must be held accountable for their results—the organizational structure must support this principle.

There are some basic principles of proper organization relating to the goal of enabling the organization to perform all required (value-added) activities in the most economical, efficient, and effective manner possible. When an organization is first started, a limited number of personnel can accomplish this. As the organization grows and the span of control exceeds the grasp of these individuals, then other employees should join the organization. However, additional employees should never be added unless their cost is less than the value added to the organization (this is the leverage principle of adding employees). Additional employees should multiply the effectiveness of management, the department, the function, or the activity, not merely make it easier for those in charge.

There are some basic principles of proper organization. Such principles must be considered in the internal benchmarking study team's review of the company's overall and departmental organization structure. Some of these organization principles are as follows:

- Clear lines of authority
- Proper division of duties and responsibilities
- Communication between functions—across functions, upward and downward
- Minimal use of personnel and then only as needed
- Proper delegation of responsibilities and authority
- Management able to effectively control the sphere of their operations and results
- Management and other personnel clearly understand what is expected of them and the results to be achieved
- Organization based on the principles of the three Es—economy, efficiency, and effectiveness
- The right size and type of organization for what the company's goals—organization, department, function, and activity
- Minimal (hopefully none) levels of non-value added management and operations personnel
- Organization no larger than it has to be to accomplish results

Organizations tend to build elaborate hierarchies, with the number of employees in each particular tower (e.g., manufacturing, personnel, accounting, and so on) bearing a direct relationship to the manager's or functions worth or clout in the organization—both in terms of personnel and budget allocations. If a specific manager is successful in building a sufficient budgetary and personnel empire, the swell of the masses will tend to rise up and push that manager toward the top of the organization in both compensation and power. In this type of system and mental model, the reward becomes one for personnel empire and budget building rather than one for results, such as operating the areas of responsibility in the most economic, efficient, and effective manner possible—even when this means recommending the reduction or elimination of the department, function, or activity.

We were performing an internal benchmarking study in an organization of this type, where the ticket to heaven was to make the management ranks. Once an individual was promoted to manager, he or she ceased to be evaluated effectively for results, but mainly for the size of his or her staff and the budget commanded. These individuals contributed less to the organization as managers than when they first joined the company. They spent most of their time getting in their employees' way, hindering rather than helping. If they had any time to fill, they would call a meeting which filled their time as well as their fellow managers'. As the years went by, these managers would get further away from the reality of their field and see their employees as threatening. To save themselves and their positions, they would promote from a position of safety, which resulted in the perpetuation of the cycle of mediocrity. It is these very practices that an organizational should identify and correct.

A representative top-level organization chart is shown as Exhibit 3.8, which illustrates the supposed reporting relationships from the President of the company down through departmental lines. This typical organizational structure would compare to most organizations. It is based on a hierarchical pyramid concept where the ultimate power starts at the top of the organization and is delegated (sometimes not) down through to the bottom of the pyramid. This organizational model originates from the military, whose purpose is to maintain control within the organization through a chain of command which demands obedience from each level reporting to a higher level. At present, many organizations still function in this manner, where the purpose for the organizational hierarchy is to police and control those reporting to higher levels to ensure that they are doing their jobs. If the study team can get these employees to do the right job (and do it right) on their own under a concept of motivating self-disciplined behavior, then the layers of non-value-added management are no longer needed and the organization can function better with less overall employees. This is the benchmark for organizational structures.

This organizational structure is also established with the intrinsic message that those in a higher position on the chart must know

Exhibit 3.8   Top Level Organization Chart

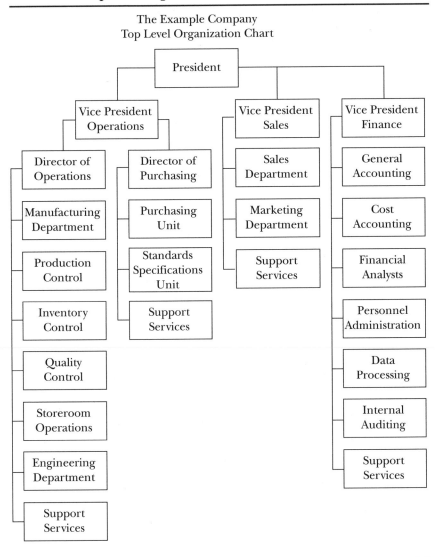

The Example Company
Top Level Organization Chart

Reprinted by permission of John Wiley & Sons, Inc. Reider, Rob. *Operational Review: Maximum Results at Efficient Costs, Second Edition*, NY: John Wiley & Sons, 1999, p. 107.

more. This mental model results in managers spending much of their time reviewing the work of those reporting to them and then having them redo it so it looks more like what they would do. It is this policing and control, and review and redo processes that make these managers superfluous and non-value-added overhead—often more hindrance than help. Encouraging self-disciplined employee behavior can eliminate many of these layers of unnecessary organization.

As the internal benchmarking team reviews and analyzes the top level organization chart in Exhibit 3.8, they may have many questions. They may identify areas for change to make the organization more effective and efficient—also more economical as a result. Some areas that the study team might question include:

- The necessity for Vice Presidents and their real functions
- The Directors' level and their purposes
- The number of functions reporting to the Vice President of Operations and the related reporting and control structures
- The number of departmental levels and breakdowns such as the manufacturing and finance areas
- Which departments or units are necessary, could be combined, could be eliminated, could be provided more economically in another manner
- Reporting relationships throughout the organization such as between the President and Vice Presidents, the Vice Presidents and Directors, and so on
- The degree of value-added management and supervision, as opposed to policing and control, and review and redo procedures
- The ability of personnel to perform their functions in a motivated self-disciplined mode without the need for close supervision or management
- The purpose of support services for each branch of the organization
- Why each area of operations is organized in a hierarchical structure rather than other possibilities such as participative

management, team management, no management, a coaching and facilitating structure and so on
- Why each function, such as inventory control and storeroom operations, needs its own organization structure rather than some other means of providing the function

If management can not effectively control the sphere of their operations and results, there will be no understanding by management and other personnel as to what is expected of them and the results to be achieved. The organization will not be established on the principles of economy, efficiency, and effectiveness.

The organization chart for the operations area is shown in Exhibit 3.9. This chart shows a further breakdown of the functional areas reporting to the Vice President of Operations. The internal benchmarking team's review of this organization chart, paying special attention to the purchasing function, reveals some areas for further review and change, such as the following:

- Why does the Purchasing Department report to the Vice President of Operations?
- What are functions, responsibilities, and authority of staff functions such as Market Analyst and Administrative Analyst? Are they value-added or non-value-added?
- Why are two Clerk Stenographers reporting directly to the Vice President of Operations? What do they do? Are they necessary?
- What is the function and authority of the Purchasing Supervisor? (Note: This position was listed as Director of Purchasing on the top level organization chart.)
- What are the Buyer II and Buyer I functions and how are they used?
- What is the difference between a Buyer II and a Buyer I?
- Are all of the seven buyers necessary, based on a division of the workload?

Exhibit 3.9 Breakdown of Functional Areas Reporting to the Vice President of Operations

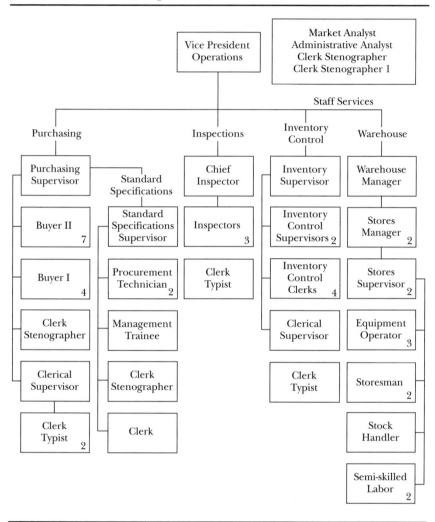

Reprinted by permission of John Wiley & Sons, Inc. Reider, Rob. *Operational Review: Maximum Results at Efficient Costs, Second Edition*, NY: John Wiley & Sons, 1999, p. 108.

- What is the function of the Purchasing Department Clerk Stenographer and how does this differ from the Clerical Supervisor and Clerk Typists?
- What does the Clerical Supervisor do? Is such supervision necessary?
- What are the functions of the two Clerk Typists and is the workload appropriate?
- What is the function of the Standards Specifications Unit? Is it necessary?
- Is the personnel complement within the Standards Specifications Unit appropriate?
- What are the specific functions of the Standards Specifications Unit personnel?
- How much purchasing activity is really necessary? Based on this reduced level of activity, what should be the appropriate organization structure and personnel complement be?

We were performing an internal benchmarking study at a fairly large national corporation. During the course of our review of the company's organizational structure, the study team identified the practice of departmental organizational empire and budget building. It was apparent that each operating division had built up a support staff which far exceeded the work demands. The organization was so top heavy that we called it the "leaning tower of appeasement." Management was profiting while the number of employees reporting to them kept increasing with minimal value-added efforts.

While sales and cost of sales had remained fairly steady, general and administrative costs had skyrocketed to over 300 percent from just two years ago. After some analysis work, the study team determined that the cause for such a large rise in administrative costs was the philosophy of the new company President, which was to reward managers so that they would be loyal and productive. As the study team learned, these managers were indeed loyal, as long as the rewards kept coming. However, the only results they produced were personal perquisites such as club memberships, upgraded company cars, first class travel, and so on.

The employees who reported to these managers became cohesive against management and as a result accomplished as little as possible. The managers had become cohesive as well, supporting each other in a covenant to maintain their status quo. After some time, the President was replaced in an effort to control costs. The new President downsized almost all of the managers out of existence with minimal impact upon operations. In the short term, productivity increased greatly as employee morale increased. However, in the longer term, the situation sunk back to where it was as these employees still received no additional rewards or compensation for their additional efforts and results.

The internal benchmarking team recommended the implementation of a compensation system which was based on compensating for results, rather than for seniority or position with responsibility on the part of the employees requiring less managers and more coaches and facilitators. This best practice provided for the least organization with the most results.

The internal benchmarking team can use various organizational review tools to gather and analyze information about the organization and to identify areas for improvement. Usually, these tools are combined with data provided directly by management and operations personnel (user provided data) and data developed by the study team (analytically provided data). A sample tool is an organizational survey form, as shown in Exhibit 3.10., which stresses organizational concerns and management roles and responsibilities.

Exhibit 3.10　Organizational Survey Form

Planning

1. How does the company plan? Describe the system of planning.
2. Does a long-range plan exist? If so, attach copy.
3. Do current short-term plans exist? If so, attach copy.
4. What are the plans for expansion or improvement? How will they impact on the organization?
5. What are the plans for physical plant development? How will they impact on the organization?

Exhibit 3.10   *(Continued)*

6. What are personnel plans?
   - Positions to be added
   - Positions to be eliminated
   - Functions to be changed
7. How does the organization budget? Does it encourage the increase of personnel costs and positions? Are personnel positions and costs part of the budget justification process?

Personnel and Staffing

1. Does an organization chart exist? If so, provide copy.
2. Do job descriptions exist for each block on the organization chart? If so, provide copies.
3. Are job descriptions of a general nature by position, or do they involve specific functional descriptions for each employee?
4. Do staffing statistics by functional area exist? If so, provide copies. Are there areas where such statistics do not exist?
5. How are employees recruited, screened, interviewed, and hired? Document.
6. Is there a system of employee evaluations? Describe.
7. Is there a process for justifying a new position? Describe.
8. How are employees oriented and trained? Describe.
9. What are salary increase and promotional policies? Describe.
10. How are salary increases (and decreases) determined? Who makes these decisions?
11. Is there an employee personnel manual? Obtain a copy.
12. Is there a wage and salary policy and adopted schedule? Is it shared with employees? Obtain a copy.
13. Is there an employee grievance procedure? Describe.
14. What types of personnel records are maintained? Document.
15. Are staffing patterns established based on operational requirements justified by the three Es or by some other means? Describe.
16. Are employees cross-trained or do they remain in the same area throughout their employment with the company?

(continues)

Exhibit 3.10 *(Continued)*

17. Are personnel adequately capable and competent for their jobs?
18. How are employees disciplined, laid off, and fired? Describe.

Management

1. Is there a Board of Directors? If so, provide list of names, addresses, and credentials?
2. What are the functions of the Board? How often does it meet?
3. Who is considered top management? Provide list of names.
4. Who is considered middle management? Provide list of names.
5. Who is considered lower management (supervision)? Provide list of names.
6. How adequate are existing reports in furnishing information for making management decisions? Document.
7. Are there internal downward communication tools to the staff? Describe.
8. Are authority and related responsibilities effectively delegated to management and lower levels? Describe.
9. Is there an effective mechanism for upward communications—from the staff to levels of management? Describe.
10. Is management performing its function of managing entrusted resources in the most economical, efficient, and effective manner? Describe how this is accomplished.
11. What is the criteria for management promotion? Describe system.
12. Are managers effectively evaluated as to achieving desired results using minimal scarce resources? Describe system.

Authority and Responsibility

1. Has authority been delegated effectively to managers and lower levels within the organization? Describe the process.
2. Are responsibilities clearly defined and understood by managers and staff personnel? Describe the process.
3. Are there written policies and procedures relating to personnel and other functions? If so, provide copies.
4. Do employees know what is expected of them and exactly what authority and responsibility have been assigned to them?

Exhibit 3.10 *(Continued)*

5. Do managers and employees understand the difference between authority and responsibility? Explain and provide examples.

6. Are there any instances where authority has not been delegated to the lowest level possible? Document.

7. Are there any instances where managers tasks that could be more effectively accomplished at a lower level? Document such instances.

8. Are there any instances where managers and employees perform the same tasks (e.g., review and redo)? Document such instances.

9. Are there any areas where managers appear to be superfluous? Document such areas.

10. Are there any areas where you believe that self-motivated disciplined behavior would be more effective than formal management? Document these areas.

11. Does power and control rise upward throughout the organization? Describe the process.

12. Are responsibilities properly assigned? Note any areas of overload or underload and unbalanced workloads.

Note: When completing this organizational survey form or having client personnel provide the responses, make sure that answers encompass the entire organization, individual departments, specific job positions, and individuals performing each function. All exceptions to the norms should be noted.

Systems Flowcharts

Another technique widely used in internal benchmarking study operational reviews is system flowcharting. The purpose of systems flowcharting is to document general and specific procedures to help the study team understand operations and activities. Flowcharts show the work actually performed, who is doing it, and how. Flowcharting provides far more satisfactory results than reviewing operating manuals and documentation because the study team gains a better and more accurate understanding of operating activities. In addition, the process of flowcharting requires obtaining and documenting an understanding of operating systems, stimulating the study team's interest, enthusiasm, and imagination. resulting in more realistic weaknesses and areas for change being identified.

The systems flowchart is a graphical representation of the sequence of operations in a process. It is especially useful in showing where documents, equipment, reference materials, files, or new paperwork enter the process. It documents what work is performed and how. Although the internal benchmarking team usually develops the systems flowchart as part of its study, it is an effective tool that management and operations personnel can use on an ongoing basis to understand the workings of their activities for analysis and operational improvements.

A possible system flowchart for the internal benchmarking study for the purchasing-receivable-payables-disbursement system is shown in Exhibit 3.11.

The systems flowchart shown in Exhibit 3.11. provides information to the internal benchmarking team relative to:

- How operations are actually carried out
- The necessity or usefulness of the work steps included in processing the transactions
- The effectiveness of the controls the process provides.

The systems flowchart also helps the internal benchmarking team to identify the system's inefficiencies such as:

- Unnecessary handling
- Inefficient routing
- Unused information on documents or records
- Inadequate planning or delegation
- Inadequate instruction
- Insufficient or excessive equipment
- Poor use of computer systems
- Poorly planned reports
- Inadequate or improper scheduling
- Uneven distribution of work
- Unnecessary, redundant, or duplicate work steps

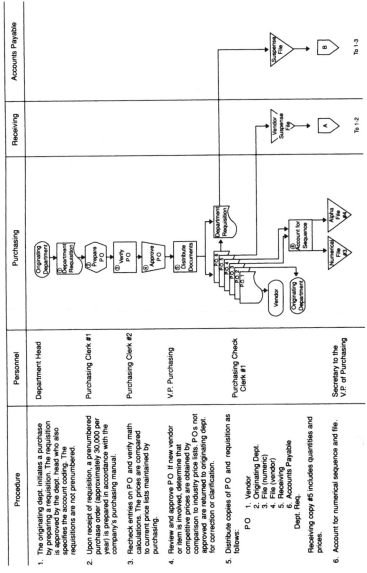

Exhibit 3.11 Systems Flowchart: Purchasing-Receiving-Payables-Disbursement System

Reprinted by permission of John Wiley & Sons, Inc. Reider, Rob. *Operational Review: Maximum Results at Efficient Costs, Second Edition*, NY: John Wiley & Sons, 1999.

Purchasing—Receiving—Payables—Disbursements System

Procedure	Personnel	Receiving	Production Control	Accounts Payable
7. When goods are received, count and check for damaged items. (See separate narrative write-up.) Prepare, sign, and date three part-prenumbered receiving report. Attach to bill of lading and P.O 5.	Receiving Clerk #1			

8. Review and compare receiving report, bill of lading and P.O 5 for completeness and any discrepancies. Distribute as follows:
  P.O 5. Production Control
  B of L. Production Control
  R.R. 1. Production Control
     2. Accounts Payable
     3. Head of receiving dept.
	Receiving Clerk #2			

Note: the two receiving clerks may rotate steps 7 and 8 as both are involved.				
9. Check numerical sequence of receiving report. Prepare daily listing of receiving reports and forward to accounts payable.	Head of Receiving Dept.			
10. Update inventory records. (See separate flowchart on inventory system for detailed discussion.)	Inventory Control Clerk #1			

Exhibit 3.11 *(Continued)*

102

Procedure	Personnel	Accounts Payable	Orig. Dept.

11. Match all related documents and hold in suspense file pending receipt of vendor invoice.

Accounts Payable Clerk #1

12. Vendor invoices are forwarded from the mail room daily. Duplicate invoices are stamped as such. Match vendor invoices with other documentation.

Accounts Payable Clerk #1

13. Review file of unmatched invoices and receiving reports daily. Notify V.P. Purchasing of unmatched items over 10 days old for his follow-up.

Head of Accounts Payable Dept.

14. Approve invoice for payment when all documents have been received and matched. Exceptions are brought to the attention of the head of Accounts Payable Dept., who is responsible for corrective action. Upon resolution, the documents are returned to the head of the originating department for approval.

Head of Originating Dept.

Exhibit 3.11 *(Continued)*

103

Procedure	Personnel	Accounts Payable	Cash Disbursements
15. Match invoice and supporting documentation to related entry on daily listing of goods received and indicate that items have been matched by initialing the list. Check all documentation, verify math computations, agree quantities, check for proper discount, verify account distribution, check for approval, and indicate work by initials. At end of month, prepare accrual on the basis of open items on daily receipts list.	Accounts Payable Clerk #2		
16. Prepare prenumbered voucher (approximately 35,000 per year). Includes all information necessary for posting to accounting records and preparation of check by E.D.P. Accumulate net amount of vouchers on adding machine tape as a control total for each day's transactions. A supply of prenumbered checks is given to computer operator.	Cash Disbursement Clerk #2		

Exhibit 3.11 *(Continued)*

104

Procedure	Personnel	EDP
E.D.P. documentation consists of the source programs, operator instructions and record layouts.		
17. The vouchers are entered via data terminal in E.D.P. An interactive edit routine is performed as data are entered.	Data Terminal Operator	
18. Computer operator processes data file through an edit program. The edit program checks that all numeric fields are numeric and checks for missing voucher numbers. The conversion process is verified by the use of record counts. Any vouchers that are detected as errors are returned to cash disbursements clerk #1. The voucher is corrected within two days and sent back to E.D.P. for reprocessing.	Computer Operator (all operators are capable of running this series of programs)	
19. The daily transaction data file is used to prepare the checks and the check register. In addition, a month-to-date transaction file of checks issued is maintained to accumulate and prepare the monthly posting to the general ledger by account. The data file has internal header and trailer labels that are tested by the program. The daily transaction data file and the month-to-date file are maintained for one week. The final MTD file is kept for 13 months.	Computer Operator	
20. End of the month procedure: The end of month file is processed to prepare a summary of the checks issued, which serves as the source document to post the journal entry in the general ledger.	Computer Operator	

Exhibit 3.11 *(Continued)*

105

Procedure	Personnel	Accounts Payable		Mail Room

Procedure	Personnel
21. The daily adding machine tape control total of vouchers is compared and reconciled to the check register. The check sequence is accounted for.	Cash Disbursement Clerk #1
22. At end of month journal entry is prepared based on summary report prepared by E.D.P. J.E. is not approved.	Cash Disbursement Clerk #2
23. Invoices and supporting documentation are collected with the voucher and checks.	Cash Disbursement Clerk #1
24. Sign checks using facsimile plate. Checks over $10,000 require manual signatures of two executives (Chairman, President, VP Finance, VP Operations).	Secretary to V.P. Finance
25. Review checks and supporting documentation, noting payee amount, approvals, and manual signatures as required.	Accounting Supervisor
26. Checks and supporting documents filed as follows: Voucher * Vendor File	Cash Disbursement Clerk #2

```
                     Check    1  Mail Room
                              2 * Vendor file
                              3  File alpha
                              4  File numeric
                     Inv.     1 * Vendor file
                              2  Mail Room
                     R.R.     1 * Vendor file
                     R.R.     2  •  •  •  •  •
                     B of L      •  •  •  •  •
                     P.O. 5      •  •  •  •  •
                     P.O. 6      •  •  •  •  •
                     Dept. Req
                     *Cancel and file by vendor
```

Exhibit 3.11 *(Continued)*

106

The detailed operating procedures demonstrated in the systems flowchart example do not represent recommended procedures, but rather procedures that an internal benchmarking team might uncover in an operational review. Consequently, the study team's focus should not be on these detailed procedures, but on how the flowchart is structured to identify strengths and weaknesses in the operations by classifying procedures by departments and relating their flow across departmental lines. Although it is important that the study team knows how to prepare systems flowcharts, it is equally important for them to know how to analyze them. In this context, review the systems flowchart in Exhibit 3.11 and try to analyze the process and identify possible deficiencies, questionable items, and areas for additional examination that might be critical to the operation. Suggested responses are shown in Exhibit 3.12.

Exhibit 3.12   Analysis of Systems Flowchart Suggested Responses

1a. Question whether the Department Heads should be coding accounts on purchase requisitions. Is this the best use of a manager's time? This may also be a tip of the iceberg situation, where an organizational pattern (or mental model) exists where management personnel perform clerical tasks.

1b. Are purchase requisitions really needed? And if so, are they needed in the present number? If purchase requisitions can be eliminated, the getting ready, filling out, distribution and handling, and putting away are also eliminated. The purpose of the purchase requisition is to notify central purchasing to process a purchase. If a large number of purchases can be accomplished in a more effective and efficient manner and others can be processed automatically through purchasing, then the company can eliminate the purchase requisition process for those items.

1c. Purchase requisitions are not pre-numbered. Numerical control over purchase requisitions ensures that the Purchasing Department processes all purchases and processes no requisitions more than once. The presence of computers should eliminate all such document transfer in favor of electronic transfer.

(continues)

Exhibit 3.12 *(Continued)*

2. Purchasing Clerk annually prepares approximately 30,000 purchase orders. This is a large number of purchase orders in general, especially for one person to handle. The universe of purchase orders should be analyzed to determine which ones can be eliminated, combined, processed automatically, and so on. Only those items requiring purchasing review prior to purchasing should remain for processing.

3a. Another Purchasing Clerk rechecks entries on the purchase order and verifies math calculations. The computer system usually prepares purchase orders (where necessary) automatically. This step should be eliminated. This may be another tip of the iceberg situation, where computer systems are available but not properly used.

3b. The prices are compared to current price lists the Purchasing Department maintains. How are these prices maintained, kept accurate and up-to-date? This should be computerized, eliminating the bulk of manual efforts.

4a. The Vice President of Purchasing reviews and approves all purchase orders. This, again, is not the best use of management time—a non-value-added activity. Determine the necessity for this position.

4b. If a new vendor or item is involved, the Vice President determines that competitive prices are obtained. Again, a function that a Vice President does not need to perform.

4c. Unapproved purchase orders are returned to the originating department for correction or clarification. With the reduction and combination of purchase orders and the use of electronic and automatic ordering, only a minimal number of purchase orders would remain. There is no reason why any of these would be returned to the originating department.

4d. There is no mention of whether purchases agree to approved plans and budgets. If so, the purchase should be automatic. It is the material on the purchase that is verified to the plans and budget, not the amount. If the amount differs, it should be an automatic budget adjustment within the framework of flexible budget concepts.

5. Distribute copies of purchase order and purchase requisition.

5a. The Purchase Requisition should be returned to the issuer as proof of processing and not returned to accounts payable. A computer message will eliminate the paper.

Exhibit 3.12 *(Continued)*

5b. The originating department needs to receive notification of their open purchases, but not necessarily a copy of the purchase order. With a computer system, this could take the form of an open purchase data file. Best practices call for the elimination of all unnecessary paperwork and manual processing where computer systems are available.

5c. Two copies of the purchase order (one maintained in numeric sequence and one in alphabetic sequence) are kept in the Purchasing Department. The computer system should eliminate all of this paper, filing, seeking, and re-filing.

5d. The Receiving Department normally receives notification of open purchases to be received. In this case, they are using a copy of the purchase order. Again, a computer data file of open (unreceived) purchases would serve much better. There is no reason to have prices on the file. This is an area for investigating best practices—internally and externally.

6. The secretary to the Vice President of Purchasing accounts for the numerical sequence of the purchase orders and files both the numerical and alphabetical copies. This is an unnecessary operation with proper computer systems. Question the purpose of the Vice President of Purchasing and the secretary.

7a. Question the amount of damaged items in the damaged items procedure. This may indicate some problem vendors. If these damaged items can be eliminated or greatly reduced, it also eliminates the need for elaborate procedures.

7b. Preparation of a three-part receiving report. Good business practice is never to re-record information that already exists in the system. In this instance, receiving data already is shown on the purchase order copy and should be considered the receiving report. As a best practice, this data should come automatically from the computer system.

8. Review and compare receiving report and purchase order copy. With the use of the purchase order itself or a computer system, there is no need for this work step.

9. Check the numerical sequence of receiving reports and have the head of the Receiving Department prepare a daily listing of receiving reports. This step would also be eliminated.

(continues)

Exhibit 3.12 *(Continued)*

10. Update inventory records. At present, this is done on a manual basis, independent of other updating. This inventory updating should be integrated and simultaneously processed under a computer system.

11. Match all related documents and hold in suspense file pending receipt of vendor invoices. This step is necessary at present, but notice the number of documents already accumulated in the process—many of which should be eliminated. A properly designed computer system will eliminate this manual suspense file.

12. The mailroom forwards vendor invoices. This procedure should be reviewed to determine if this is the most efficient way of receiving and processing vendor invoices. Effective alternatives might be for the accounts payable department to receive vendor invoices directly or via a lock-box system. Other possible best practices include direct electronic vendor payments at the time of receipt (as part of vendor negotiations and pricing) or subsequent electronic payment after receipt. It might be possible to eliminate the manual accounts payable altogether or greatly reduce it.

13. Review of unmatched invoices and receiving reports. With a properly designed computer system, this function is done automatically for timely follow-up. At present, it is not a function that the Head of Accounts Payable needs to be involved with, nor does the Vice President of Purchasing.

14a. Approve invoice for payment. This is a necessary step, however it should be an exception. All of those the computer system can match should be automatically processed for payment based on programmed in payment timings. Note the number of documents to be reviewed and filed at present. All of these can be eliminated.

14b. Exceptions brought to the attention of the head of accounts payable for corrective action. Determine the nature and number of such exceptions. There should be minimal exceptions which can be clerically corrected. If a large number or a consistent type of exception persists, it indicates that the correction addresses the symptom rather than the cause of the problem.

14c. Upon resolution, the documents return to the Head of the Originating Department for approval. This step is unnecessary, as are the documents.

15a. Matching invoice and support documentation and verifying math, discount, account distribution, and so forth. This is a perfect

Exhibit 3.12   *(Continued)*

computer application. Attempt to get as much data in electronic form rather than relying on keying in of data.

15b. End of month accrual based on open items on daily receipt list. Computer system should provide this automatically.

16a. Prepare pre-numbered voucher (approximately 35,000 annually). As the purpose of the voucher is to provide the necessary data in an orderly manner for subsequent data entry, there is no need for this work step or the documents involved if the data already exists within the computer system.

16b. Review data entry control procedures so that data entry is kept to a minimum and the computer system provides the most efficient method for controlling.

This is the first indication in the process that computer systems are in existence. The study team should determine the extent of computer procedures, the overall capability of present computer resources, the effectiveness of its use, and the efficient use for present systems concerns. In this situation, the study team might recommend the increased use of computer procedures for the present system under review to provide for the economies, efficiencies, and effectiveness already discussed.

Review the accumulated supporting documents. As can be seen, the present systems have created an enormous amount of manual processing and paperwork necessary for the purchasing, receiving, payables, and vendor payment functions. Each document and its related manual processing that can be eliminated results in the reduction of personnel costs, forms cost, preparation costs, handling time, filing time and costs, and so on. Best practices and effective computerization can eliminate (or greatly reduce) all of these.

The Stockton Specialty Products Company engaged a group of computer consultants to design and implement a management information system to meet their needs. The consultants installed a microcomputer local area network with data terminal access on each manager's desk. The consultants also designed an elaborate software system to provide all of the management information that any manager would ever need. The system was so elaborate that many of the managers stopped using it because they were overwhelmed with information and totally confused. The President of the company told the internal benchmarking team that the company had paid over $200,000 for a computer system that could not make a decision. They were still using their old dart board.

The internal benchmarking team looked at the systems as designed and implemented. They had to agree that the system was working as intended. However, the system was so full of information, there was a data overload. It was no wonder that the managers were confused and could not make a decision. All of the necessary information was included as part of the system databases, however there was no way to distinguish where to make decisions.

The internal benchmarking team, using the existing system with modifications, developed a reporting system which showed only those key operating indicators where action was necessary. The detail data was left for referral or use by operating employees. The computer consulting group's error was to impress management with all of the data available, rather than just that data required for decisions. They didn't understand the basic business principle that it is not the computer that makes the decision, the computer only provides the necessary information for others to make the decisions.

Layout Flowchart

The layout flowchart is a schematic diagram of the existing or proposed physical arrangement of a work area, to which has been added the flow lines of the principal work performed there. This type of chart is used to document the existing layout and paths of movement of people, paperwork, or materials.

The layout flowchart also enables the benchmarker to disclose certain inefficiencies in the system, such as:

- Unnecessary handling
- Inefficient routing
- Inadequate planning or delegation of work
- Inadequate instruction to employees

- Excess management, supervision, and non-value-added functions
- Insufficient or excessive personnel and equipment
- Poor use of computer systems
- Poorly planned, inefficient, or disorganized work areas
- Bad work scheduling
- Inefficient work area layout
- Cumbersome or cluttered work flow
- Outdated or outmoded furniture and fixtures

The layout flowchart also assists the benchmark team in identifying certain potential personnel roadblocks to economical, efficient, and effective operations. Among these, are:

- **Isolates.** These individuals or work units appear to be unconnected to the rest of the work area or activities.
- **Controllers.** These individuals' major function appears to be controlling or overseeing the work of others without any appreciable value added.
- **Dispatchers.** The main purpose of these individuals or work units is to receive work from one work unit or individual and pass it to another work unit or individual without appreciably adding to the work.

In addition, the benchmarking team should be aware of hierarchical pyramids, where there is a reporting relationship either upward or downward, and where the individuals in the pyramid appear to be mainly reviewing and/or redoing (or having the employee redo) the work passed to them prior to passing it further up or down the pyramid. Most organizational pyramids are constructed so that each higher level can police and control the lower level, while many times providing no other value-added benefits than to ensure that the lower levels do their work. If these hierarchical levels can be eliminated, it can greatly reduce the cost of operations without sacrificing results (many times results will increase). What is really necessary is to motivate each worker's self-disciplined work behavior, in effect making the workers responsible for their own and the work group's results.

Present Layout Flow Diagram. A layout flow diagram for a representative manufacturing facility as documented in an internal benchmarking study is shown in Exhibit 3.13. Some areas of inefficiency, bottlenecks, poor working conditions, poor work flow, unnecessary activities, and so on were identified by the study team as follows:

- Six work centers; one for specialty products, one for custom products, two for defense work, and two for basic board products; causing uneven distribution of work load and non-prioritized allocation of space.
- Six-member work teams not always necessary. All customer orders for any one of the product lines are set up in this manner. However, in most instances fewer personnel and work steps are necessary. For example, only two work steps are required for the production of basic boards.
- Packing, shipping, and receiving are merging into each other's work areas. It is quite difficult to determine what is coming in and what is going out.
- Inventory; raw materials, work in process, and finished goods are stored about the production floor making it difficult to determine which is which.
- Quality Control is performing off-line inspections which delays the production process for each customer order. In addition, Quality Control is housed away from the production area in the office area.
- The presence of six forepersons and six team leaders results in these individuals getting in each other's way (as well as the production workers), rather than enhancing productivity.
- The amount of unnecessary inventory coupled with the lack of sufficient storage space has resulted in physical inventory getting in the way of production, inability to find specific items, and lack of overall inventory control.

Exhibit 3.13 Present Layout Flow Diagram

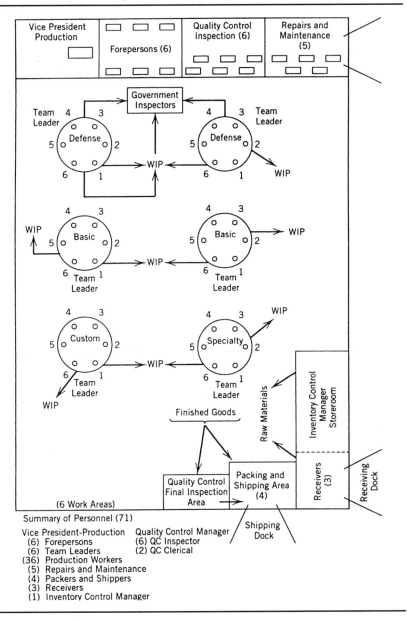

Summary of Personnel (71)

Vice President-Production   Quality Control Manager
(6) Forepersons   (6) QC Inspector
(6) Team Leaders   (2) QC Clerical
(36) Production Workers
(5) Repairs and Maintenance
(4) Packers and Shippers
(3) Receivers
(1) Inventory Control Manager

Reprinted by permission of John Wiley & Sons, Inc. Reider, Rob. *Operational Review: Maximum Results at Efficient Costs, Second Edition*, NY: John Wiley & Sons, 1999.

Observation of Production Operations. The internal benchmarking team found that the company had recently (less than six months ago) moved into a new production facility in a brand-new industrial park. However, the company has not taken advantage of the increased space. Already, production facilities are cramped, with the six work centers encroaching upon one another. In addition, with the increase in inventory, many parts are spread around the production facility, not only overcrowding needed production facilities, but also making it difficult to control physical inventory.

Quality Control, which should be an integral part of production, is housed in the office area. This makes it difficult to find quality control personnel when needed. In addition, quality control personnel are forced to conduct their testing on an off-line basis in a separate room at the far end of the manufacturing facility. It would be more economical and efficient to conduct necessary quality control testing directly on-line in the work centers.

The receiving, packing, and shipping areas which were intended to be separate activities have been forced together creating enormous confusion as to what is coming in and what is going out. These employees are presently working right on top of each other.

Inventory was intended to be minimal, to be ordered "just in time" for a customer order going into production. This is not working as raw materials (mainly standard printed circuit boards for the various types of products) are stacked everywhere. The inventory control manager does not appear to be sure what is on-hand and orders additional quantities of existing inventory.

The bulk of the finished goods inventory for specialty, custom, and defense products are supposed to be shipped out by customer order as completed. However, there is an enormous amount of such finished goods in inventory, where quite possibly the same items are being manufactured.

Each of the six work centers consists of six work stations for standard operations:

1. Initial set-up
2. Component placement

116

3. Wiring
4. Soldering
5. Completion
6. Final testing

The internal benchmarking team observed that for most specialty and custom board customer orders these six steps are unnecessary. Generally, initial set-up and component placement can be combined, the same worker can do wiring and soldering, completion remains the same, and quality control inspectors should do the final testing (maybe the only quality control inspection). The company should get out of the defense business as it takes up needed production space but doesn't contribute greatly to sales or profits. The basic board business is mainly one of purchase and resale and doesn't need to be part of the manufacturing facility as these boards can be purchased and outside vendors can ship them directly more economically and efficiently.

Proposed Product Line Manufacturing Observations. The main production facility should be devoted to specialty and custom board manufacturing. Production jobs should be based on realistic sales forecasts and/or real customer orders. Through the efforts and coordination of the engineering and sales departments, standardization of products should be maximized. This will allow scheduling more jobs by product rather than by customer, providing efficiencies of material ordering, inventory control, production scheduling and control, shop floor control, and the ability to deliver on-time.

The manufacturing process should also be analyzed for each specialty and custom product so that the most efficient methods of production and the smallest number of work steps need to be considered. The production layout can then be set up on a flexible basis considering the various possibilities (e.g., two work steps or four work steps) and mix of products at any one time.

Through the elimination of the defense business, the present space allocated to this product line can be reallocated for increased specialty and custom board production. In addition, the conversion of the basic board business to a sales distribution type business frees up additional production space. To the extent the company can have their vendors ship directly to basic board customers, additional space will become available.

Proposed Plant Layout Flow Diagram. The proposed plant layout flow diagram which incorporates the internal benchmarking team's findings and implementation of best practices is shown in Exhibit 3.14.

Fifteen features and basic assumptions of the proposed plant layout which make it most effective include the list below. Remember, these are best practice changes based on an internal benchmarking study. Additional internal review or an external benchmarking study will produce further improvements and best practices. In addition, it is expected that operations personnel will enhance these implemented best practices as part of a program of continuous improvements.

1. The capability to schedule production to the extent possible by product or finished good part number through standardization and the ability to separate out add-on options.
2. Flexibility in production as to the type of processes and number of work steps. The proposed layout is set up for a three-step and a two-step process. However, any combination of work steps and quality control inspections can be set up based on the needs of the product.
3. Use of production personnel based on the job to be manufactured. To be most effective, each worker should be flexible as to what tasks or activities he or she can perform—that is cross training.
4. Effective use of three floating trainer/coaches who would help and facilitate each worker to do what he or she does best even better, help other workers learn from each other, and improve areas where specific workers may need additional help.
5. Use of a plant manager to ensure that everything gets done correctly and on-time from a helping and problem-solving

Exhibit 3.14 Proposed Plant Layout Flow Diagram

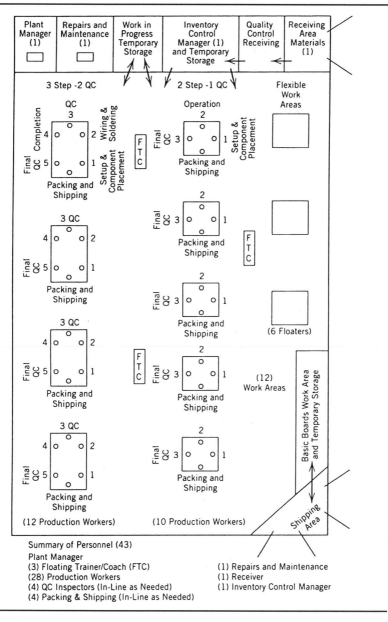

Reprinted by permission of John Wiley & Sons, Inc. Reider, Rob. *Operational Review: Maximum Results at Efficient Costs, Second Edition,* NY: John Wiley & Sons, 1999.

standpoint rather than as a disciplinarian—fix the problem, not the blame.

6. Quality control inspectors to be part of the production schedule and the production process, with the ability to move from job to job as needed without delaying the production process.

7. Packers and shippers to work together on-line with the production teams so that as parts are finished, they can be packed and routed to shipping for immediate customer delivery.

8. The production schedule to take into account periods of under- and over-capacity conditions with the company able to plan and make effective decisions. When additional production facility is needed (more work than can be handled or over capacity) the company could network with other electronics manufacturers to pick up the slack at previously agreed on terms, develop a network of ex-employees and others to come in part-time, use flexible scheduling to increase production at minimal additional cost, and so on. For under-capacity conditions (not enough work to fill the plant capacity), the company could consider having the six floaters as part-time or contractors, negotiate to perform work for others, attempt to bring projected sales in earlier, and so on.

9. Getting out of the defense business and developing the basic board business as a sales distribution business, with the vendor shipping a large amount of such basic board sales directly to the customer.

10. Coordinating customer sales with basic boards ordered from vendors, deliveries from vendors, and customer delivery schedules. In other words, have the vendor hold the company's inventory and either ship directly to the customer or deliver to the company, based on the customer's delivery schedule. This allows the company to get out of the basic board inventory business with only a temporary storage area needed.

11. Effectively control work in process so that no production jobs sit in production for any length of time (e.g., no more than one day of planned production queue time) and customer delivery schedules are met. This will provide for minimum work in process in a temporary storage area, which can be better controlled and managed.

12. Maintaining only one regular repair and maintenance employee to handle necessary and emergency tool and equipment repairs. Other tool repairs should be sent to the outside or the tools replaced. Ongoing equipment maintenance should be contracted to the outside. Regular maintenance should become the responsibility of each production employee to do.

13. Stressing specialty and custom boards as its main business, coupled with greater standardization, should allow the company to negotiate better with their vendors as to parts needed, time (vendor delivery schedules to coordinate with the company's production schedule), and level of quality (e.g., at least 98 percent). In effect, the company makes their vendors the keepers of their materials inventory until needed for production. Should the company be successful in this area, it should be able to get by with one receiver, a relatively small temporary storage area for materials, and a clean job for the inventory control manager.

14. The company might want to consider becoming a distributor for one or more of its major vendors. Typically, this approach allows the company to purchase product at a lesser cost, sometimes on consignment (not paying until used or resold) and to have materials on hand when needed. This approach will require more storage space, but it might be offset by cost savings and other benefits.

15. Through the implementation of the proposed plant layout and its underlying features and assumptions, the company should also be able to increase productivity (at least by 25 percent), work more efficiently, reduce inventory levels,

increase customer on-time deliveries and satisfaction, improve cash flow, increase employee morale, and so on.

Note that as a result of this phase of the internal benchmarking study, the study team was able to reduce the number of production employees from 71 to 43 with increased productivity, efficiencies, economies, and results. Operations personnel was responsible for implementing even greater changes and best practices to those areas changed by the new plant layout as well as other areas of operations. This is the start of a program for continuous improvement in the manufacturing area.

RECOMMENDATIONS

The successful completion of the internal benchmarking study is the development of recommendations for the action to correct undesirable conditions. Each recommendation should logically follow an explanation of why the present condition is happening, the underlying causes, and what should be done to prevent it from recurring. The recommendation should have as its basis the study team's knowledge and awareness of the best practice for the situation. Their recommendations should be practical and reasonable, so that management will easily see the merits in adopting them.

In developing their recommendations, the study team should select the best known practice for correcting the situation. The best practice can come from study team members' previous knowledge and experience, research form other sources such as periodicals and journals, observations at other organizations, outside sources such as consultants and specialists in the area, and so on. Sometimes the best recommendation for a best practice to implement comes from the operations personnel themselves. Often it is these employees who work with the function or activity day after day and know first-hand what the problem is, the cause of the problem, and the best way to correct it. Sometimes it only requires the patience of the study team to listen to these operations personnel to quickly acquire the best practice and the right solution. It is less important where the specific recommendation comes from and more important that the study team arrives at the right solution for the situation.

In formulating their recommendations, the study team must consider various factors:

- Present mental models, belief systems, and performance drivers existing in the company. If one of these is partly (or completely) the cause of the problem at hand, then the study team must work on changing it prior to implementing their recommendation. If change is not possible, then the study team can only recommend a less-than-best practice.
- Strategic plans and thrust for the company as communicated by top management. For any recommendation to be implemented most successfully, it must be congruent with management's strategic planning. Otherwise, management will be moving in one direction, while other parts of the company move in another.
- Performance drivers and performance measures as directed or dictated by management or observed and analyzed by the study team. The benchmarking team can either try to correct such elements as part of the study or try to work around them. Management may have its reasons (logical or not) for wishing to maintain a performance driver which the study team sees as a negative influence on company economy, efficiency, or effectiveness.
- The synergistic effect of changing one area of operations, as it may affect other areas. For instance, changing to a just-in-time material receipt system in manufacturing without communicating the change to the purchasing area.
- The resistance to change factor by those employees directly involved in the change as well as others whom the change affect. For instance, changing the method of compensation for sales personnel from a commission basis to a results-oriented basis. The purpose of the change may be to get the sales group more integrated with company plans and manufacturing needs. However, the sales personnel may see the

change as a way of reducing their overall compensation. The result may be less sales efforts and idle plant capacity.

• The ownership of the recommendation can also play an important part in whether operations personnel readily accepts the recommendation or subtly sabotages it in some manner. If operations personnel see the recommendation as coming from the study team and/or top management, they may work against it merely to show their opposition to being directed. On the other hand, if operations personnel believe that the recommendation is theirs (in large part or entirely), there is a greater likelihood that they will work toward successful implementation.

In developing their recommendations, the internal benchmarking team should try to answer these questions:

• What do you recommend to correct the situation?
• Is your recommendation based on a logical connection to the present practice?
• Is your recommendation practical and reasonable for implementation?
• Do the operations personnel involved with implementing the recommendation agree with the change?

Many times, a workable recommendation seems to suggest itself, but in other cases the study team may need some ingenuity to come up with a sensible recommendation that has a reasonable chance of adoption. Internal benchmarking recommendations should be as specific and helpful as possible; and not simply that operations need to be improved, controls need to be strengthened, or planning systems need to be implemented. The study team should do their best to make certain that their recommendations are practical and acceptable to those responsible for taking action.

Each recommendation should be directed to a specific management and/or operations member, so that it is clear who is responsible for the necessary action to implement the recommendation. In addition, the study team should always weigh the cost of carrying out a recommendation against its expected benefits.

As mentioned previously, the identity of substandard practices is the most critical element of the internal benchmarking study. The development of practical and reasonable recommendations to convince management to implement them is sometimes the most difficult element of the study. Good, workable recommendations are a factor of the collective internal benchmarking team's experience. The more alternative systems and procedures they know, the better the chance to arrive at the optimum recommendation.

In developing recommendations, the internal benchmarking team should consider all sources such as study team members, outside consultants, departmental personnel, other employees, other company staff, other organizations, professional associations and members thereof, and so on. Remember, in considering and developing recommendations, the company is moving toward best practices and a program of continuous improvements.

It is less important where the recommendation comes from, and more important that it meets these desired criteria. Many times the best recommendations come from operating personnel, who only need the internal benchmarking team's channel of communication for decision-making management to hear them. In these instances, the study team must make sure that such operating personnel are given credit for identifying and/or developing the recommendation.

The more involved operations personnel are in developing recommendations, the more committed they will be to make them work most effectively. The study team's goal is to identify the systems and procedures for recommendation (best practices) that will optimize savings and be the least costly, the most efficient to use, and achieve maximum results, regardless of where they come from.

The internal benchmarking team also needs to be aware that management might turn around and ask them to assist in implementing their recommendations. Whether this is possible in a given situation, the team should use this as a test for their recommendations—"if we are asked to implement our recommendations, would we be able to do it?" If the team adequately documents their recommendations, the process for implementation, and the results to be expected, there is a good chance for success.

However, if recommendations are stated in general terms, not only will management tend to shy away from them, but there is a good chance of sabotaging results by management as well as operations personnel. The internal benchmarking team should work toward developing a working-together atmosphere with management and operating personnel in which the team's role becomes one of helping and changing. In such a working relationship, there is a much greater likelihood that management and operations personnel will accept the recommendations.

Sometimes the internal benchmarking team must temper their specific systems recommendation with personnel recommendations or required changes. For instance, an internal benchmarking team performed a study of the Purchasing Department of a fairly large organization. The study team was particularly interested in the buying function, which consisted of eight employees; and the purchase order processing and control function of five employees. The study team had each employee fill out a questionnaire as to what they believed their job responsibilities and functions were. They then interviewed each employee and observed a few days of each employee's actual activities. They verified activity and item counts for purchases made and purchase orders processed, as well as reviewing the work loads sitting in backlog. The item counts for all employees were way below the numbers claimed on the questionnaire forms. However, the number of items for each employee waiting to be processed was immense, over a week's volume based on current levels of activity. Based on the study team's observations, they came to the conclusion that these employees were not happy in their jobs and were probably working at less than half speed.

The study team shared their observations with the Purchasing Department Manager, who seemed to be a nondescript typical organization person. The manager seemed quite surprised at the study team's observations and defended the employees as hard-working, conscientious individuals. Their volume statistics were consistently the same and quite acceptable within the company's work standard reporting system. The fact that each employee could be producing at least twice the current volume didn't seem to matter.

The study team talked with a number of the employees to determine if there was any overt or hidden sabotage against the manager. All of the employees had very little to say about the manager—they just did their jobs as they were told. About this time, the manager left for a two-week vacation. Almost immediately the work atmosphere changed. Where it was slow and tedious before, it was now humming with activity. The study team brought their observations to the head buyer and the supervisor of purchase order processing to determine if they knew what might have caused such a change. They were both as amazed as the study team at the positive change in work atmosphere and attitude, but neither one of them could claim any credit for it. One of the study team members happened to mention the change to one of the other buyers. She just smiled and said, "Don't you understand? We are free at last, the boss is gone." The study team member said, "I thought none of you disliked him." The employee shook her head, "We don't dislike him, we are just not happy working for him. He makes us feel sad."

To develop their recommendations based on a sound basis of doing the right thing and keeping it that way, the internal benchmarking team should be aware of as many benchmarks for best practices as possible. Some of these are shown in Exhibit 3.15. for the organization and by functional area.

Exhibit 3.15 Benchmarks for Best Practices

ORGANIZATION AND MANAGEMENT

1. Minimal levels of organizational structure.
2. Value-added management
3. Management by results, not by seniority
4. Management roles clearly defined
5. Each organizational function organized for its needs, not for conformity

(continues)

Exhibit 3.15   *(Continued)*

6. Clear integration of functions—not separate empires
7. Allocation or resources based on functional needs, not on power structure
8. Each necessary function organized for economy, efficiency, and effectiveness

MANUFACTURING

1. Production based on real customer orders, not on unrealistic sales forecasts
2. Production schedule based on realistic customer delivery requirements
3. Inventory levels kept to a minimum:
   - Raw material just in time from vendors at 100 percent quality
   - Work in process entered into production on time, processed on time, and completed on time for delivery to the customer.
   - Finished goods shipped directly to customers when needed at 100 percent quality
4. Manufacturing productivity maximized:
   - Set-up operations minimized or eliminated
   - Processing operations maximized as to increased productivity
   - Minimize or eliminate manufacturing support activities such as material moves, queue times, wait times.
5. Quality control reduced or eliminated:
   - Incoming inspections only as necessary (more vendor responsibility)
   - In-process inspections minimized (more operations personnel responsibility)
   - Final inspections only as necessary
6. Storeroom operations
   - Minimize facilities for raw material and finished goods
   - Minimize storing, issuing, and restorings
   - Eliminate (or reduce greatly) obsolete inventory
   - Concept of temporary storage with less (or no) storekeepers

Exhibit 3.15 *(Continued)*

7. Production management
   - Eliminate management by direction and coercion
   - Managers as coaches and facilitators rather than police
   - Self-responsibility of operations personnel

PURCHASING

1. Responsible for vendor negotiations and best purchases as to quality, timeliness, and price—not for processing purchase orders
2. Eliminate all items that can be purchased more economically and effectively by other means such as:
   - Petty cash funds
   - Cash/credit card payments
   - Direct telephone systems
   - Electronic ordering
   - Release from contracts such as blanket purchase orders
3. Efficient processing using electronic data transfer for such things as:
   - Purchase requisitions
   - Purchase orders
   - Release from purchase orders
   - Expediting with vendors
   - Control of open orders and receipts
4. Integration with other systems such as:
   - Inventory control
   - Production control
   - Receiving
   - Accounts payable

SALES DEPARTMENT

1. Sales forecasts realistic and integrated with company plans and production schedule
2. Sales related to agreed direction of company, not by sales department

(continues)

Exhibit 3.15 *(Continued)*

3. Sales made to the right customer, with the right items, at the right time

4. Sales efforts properly balanced between making sales and providing customer service

5. Sales made only to good customers where amounts due can be collected on time

6. Sales compensation program provides for directing the sales force

FINANCIAL AND ACCOUNTING

1. Minimize the levels of manual processing through computer systems, over:

   • General ledger entries—automatic from other systems

   • Cost accounting—byproduct of manufacturing control system

   • Payroll—automatic input and possibly outside processor

   • Accounts payable—automatic from purchasing and receiving systems

   • Accounts receivable—automatic from manufacturing and shipping systems

2. Minimize the level of transactions for accounts payable and receivables by:

   • Direct payments—receipt to vendors, delivery to customers

   • Electronic data transfers—no payment processing and no billing or collections

3. Reduce or eliminate those functions or activities that are no longer necessary

4. Analyze and interpret data rather than mechanically producing data

EXAMPLES OF INTERNAL BENCHMARKING RECOMMENDATIONS

The internal benchmarking team should present their conclusions and findings as to deficient practices with workable recommendations. This should be done orally and then in a more formal written reporting system, either as the team identifies deficiencies or at the end of the study. If findings are presented as they are identified, management and operations personnel can begin to remedy the situation as soon as possible. There is usually no need to wait for such implementation efforts until the end of the study. It is a good practice for the study team to present each finding orally to operations management and employees initially so that they may correct any misconceptions as well as improve on the recommendation. The more the recommendation becomes the company's and the less it stays the study team's, usually the better the chance for successful implementation. Only after there is mutual agreement on the specifics of the recommendation between the study team members and operations personnel should the recommendation be documented for final approval.

For example, the following recommendations were developed as part of an internal benchmarking team's study. Such recommendations were presented orally to management and operations personnel and documented in summary format to recap the agreement. Such documentation could take the form presented in Exhibit 3.16.

Exhibit 3.16   Internal Benchmarking Study Recommendations Recap

"As part of our internal benchmarking study, we reviewed Purchasing Department activities to identify those areas of deficiency where positive improvements could be made in terms of economy, efficiency, and effectiveness. We reviewed all known alternatives for best practices as part of the company's program for continuous improvements. The following areas for best practice operational improvement are noted for your review:

1. *Purchase Requisition Procedures*
   Purchase requisitions are not pre-numbered and effectively controlled resulting in instances where items are ordered more than once or where needed materials or services go unordered. Such purchase control should be initiated. We recommend that purchase requisition procedures be computerized and integrated with the company

(continues)

Exhibit 3.16 *(Continued)*

planning and budget system to reduce the number of purchase requisitions manually prepared. In addition, any remaining manually prepared purchase requisitions should be questioned as to their need, alternative methods of purchase (e.g., a cash or credit card system), and elimination. The elimination of all manually produced purchase requisitions should be considered as an ultimate outcome of this recommendation, resulting in more economical and efficient operations.

2. *Budgetary Controls*
   Purchase requisitions are not being checked against approved plans and budgets. Accordingly, purchases are being processed for many items within the company which knowingly exceed existing budgetary approvals. There is a combined problem in this situation; ineffective organizational planning and budget procedures (using static rather than flexible budgeting), and the lack of budgetary controls at the time of purchase requisitioning. With a fully integrated computer system, such requisitions are generated automatically by the planning and budget system with an emphasis on the items purchased and not necessarily the cost of the purchase.

3. Buyer Function
   The buying function is presently performed by seven Buyer IIs and four Buyer Is. We analyzed their functions and found that the work load is presently distributed by commodities. As a result of this procedure, there is an uneven distribution of the workload as to vendor relations and negotiations, processing of purchases, expediting of open purchases, and so on. We recommend distributing the work based on activity levels and making greater use of electronic purchasing. Through such changes, the company should be able to eliminate at least four of these positions in the short term.

4. *Competitive Bidding Procedures*
   Although your present purchasing procedures state that competitive bidding procedures must be used for each purchase over $2,000 and at least annually for repetitively ordered items, we found such procedures rarely applied. The purchasing function presently emphasizes best price only, disregarding such important considerations as quality, timeliness, vendor support, availability of materials, and so forth. We recommend that the company put less stress on competitive bidding procedures (only where necessary), and more stress on effective vendor negotiations as quality, timeliness, and price.

Exhibit 3.16   *(Continued)*

5. *Value Analysis Program*

   A value analysis program does not exist whereby purchasing analyzes the items to determine if the item needs to be purchased, if the quantity is excessive, if less expensive items can be used, and so on. Such a program should be initiated at once so that the purchasing function is effectively purchasing rather than merely processing purchase orders. We estimate that such a value analysis program can provide over $300,000 a month in purchasing savings as well as making the purchasing function more efficient. The value analysis program is a major component in the company's program for continuous improvements.

6. *Vendor Analysis*

   We found a predominant practice of habitually dealing with the same vendors. Vendor analysis is not presently being performed in an effective manner, considering such aspects as price, quality of goods, services delivered, and timeliness. In addition, many of these vendors were found to be providing deficient services and unacceptable levels of merchandise returns. This program should be started immediately as it is a necessary component in reaching the company's goals for manufacturing production and inventory efficiencies.

7. *Present Purchase Order Processing Costs*

   We determined that it presently costs approximately $75 to process a purchase order. This cost has not been calculated since operations began over 12 years ago, when it was calculated to be $11.80. Based on this calculation and the industry benchmark that purchase orders should not be issued where the cost to process the purchase is greater than 25 percent of the value of the purchase, your policy has been that all purchases over $50 go through purchasing. Based on our calculated cost of $75 and the 25 percent rule, all purchases under $300 should circumvent the purchasing system. This should result in a great reduction in processing and a decrease in personnel.

8. *Proposed Integrated Computer System*

   The computerized integrated purchasing control and management reporting system which we are proposing involves a communications process in which data are recorded initially and revised as needed, in order to support management and staff decisions for planning, operating, and controlling purchasing operations. Our conceptual design attempts to maximize the use of common data to satisfy the

(continues)

Exhibit 3.16   *(Continued)*

information requirements of company staff at various levels. It attempts to strike an economic balance between the value of the information to be carried and the cost of operating the system.

9. *Standard Specifications Unit*
    This unit was originally established when the company first started in business 12 years ago. At that time, purchasing specifications were required for all production materials, which needed to be developed from engineering bills of material. However, at this point, there are very few new products requiring new purchasing specifications and the unit is primarily responsible for maintaining existing specifications. Based on present requirements, you can accomplish the present level of activity with one technician and a part-time clerk. You might also consider outsourcing this function to be used on an as-needed basis only.

10. *Personnel Practices*
    Our review of personnel practices related to hiring, orientation, training, evaluation, promotion, and firing found no policies or procedures in existence. We found such practices implemented by individual managers/supervisors based on their own criteria and expertise. Due to these deficient practices and inconsistencies of application, employees are confused, staff and management is improperly trained, and qualified employees leave while undesirable personnel are retained. Such deficient practices need to be remedied as described in our compilation of best practices.

EXTERNAL BENCHMARKING TARGETS

As a result of the company's internal benchmarking study and operations review of the purchasing function, the study team should also identify other areas to be considered for an external benchmarking study. The company could decide to stop at the internal benchmarking study, especially if it is satisfied with results. It might include external benchmarking comparisons of best practices in their internal benchmarking study or use the internal benchmarking study as the start of their internal program for continuous improvements. When the company decides to identify other areas for external benchmarking, the study team should also include the identification of mental models, belief systems, performance drivers, and performance measures. External benchmarking targets for the purchasing function could include:

Purchase Requisitions

- Process: manual, computer, automatic by plan, eliminate
- Control: work unit, department, automatic, computer
- Account coding: manual, employee, management, computer
- Number: company, department, unit, employee, type
- Budget check: automatic, computer, manual, pre-approved
- Policy: purchasing, petty cash, direct cash, or credit card system
- Practices: traveling requisitions, inventory automatic

Purchase Orders

- Process: manual, computer, automatic, electronic data transfer, eliminate
- Number: location, department, unit, employee, vendor, type
- Open order control: employees, number, vendor, computer
- Approval: management, computer, automatic by plan
- Copies: number, manual, computer produced, electronic data storage
- Value analysis: prices, quantities, needed, vendors
- Form and distribution: number of copies, receiver, filing, eliminate hard copy
- Costs: to process, personnel, forms, expediting
- Vendor negotiations: blanket purchases, competitive analysis, quality, timeliness

Receiving Procedures

- Number: receipts, partial receipts, employees
- Process: manual, computer, bar coding, automated update, eliminate
- Receiving inspection: process, rejects by vendor/number, necessity

- Delivery data: on time by vendor, partial receipts
- Cost: employees, process, forms, per receipt

Inventory Update

- Process: manual, bar coding automatic, computer terminals
- Routing: direct production, inventory, holding area
- Integration: with production, inventory/accounting records
- Levels: reorder point/economic order quantity, zero inventory, just-in-time raw materials and finished goods
- Work in process: just-in-time production concepts, process times, schedule integrity, minimization

Accounts Payable

- Process: vendor invoices, pay on receipt, electronic data transfer, eliminate
- Invoice receipt: mail, direct, computer, electronic data transfer
- Number: employees, open vouchers, payments, checks
- Payments: total, by vendor, by type of item
- Returns: by vendor/number, process
- Discount policy: take all, ignore, negotiate in price
- Timeliness: in/out discount terms, processing
- Practices: electronic data transfer, integrated receipt/payment, pre-payments

CONCLUSION

Internal benchmarking allows a company to identify its critical problem areas and opportunities for positive improvement, maximizing the positive aspects of existing procedures and improving deficiencies with best practices. The internal benchmark study focuses on those most critical areas, identifying the cause of the problems and developing best practice solutions. Through coordinating activities of various areas, internal benchmarking achieves positive changes simultaneously. The process also allows these areas to work together in the analysis of present practices and the implementation of new systems and procedures. In this manner, all areas learn—with less reinventing—and change within the same time period. Internal benchmarking becomes the start of the company's program for continuous improvements and the beginning of becoming a learning organization.

Internal benchmarking can be a stand-alone project to identify critical problem areas and provide standardized improvements. It can also minimize the practice of reinventing good procedures which already exist in another part of the organization or which have been unsuccessful. Internal benchmarking can consist of simple comparisons between how different people perform the same task in the same area, or a comparison of performance across different work units within the company. It also provides the knowledge of operations and the identification of external benchmarking targets that are essential to the success of an external benchmarking project.

The internal benchmarking team, while performing the internal benchmarking study, works closely with management and operations personnel. The study team attempts to make internal operations personnel as much of their study as possible. This results in more thorough identification of critical problem areas, detailed understanding of operational processes, clear identification of the causes of the condition, and practical and reasonable solutions that operations personnel will successfully implement. In effect, the internal benchmarking study is operations personnel's study. For the internal benchmarking study team to be most successful, they should have trained operations personnel in internal benchmarking and operational review techniques so that when they leave the functional area, they leave the residual capability with operations personnel to continue their efforts as part of the company's program for continuous improvements.

Operations personnel can pick up on the successful implementation of best practices by developing even greater improvements, continuing to identify and implement additional best practices from within, or looking to the outside for best practices in an informal manner or as part of a formal external benchmarking study. Should the company decide to move on to a formal external benchmarking study, it can perform such a study with its own internal personnel or seek outside assistance. The procedures and techniques for conducting such a formal external benchmarking study are discussed in Chapter Four. As previously mentioned in Chapter One, the external benchmarking study can be a competitive study comparing the company's operations to best practices of its competitors, an industry study comparing its operations to industry best practices, or a best-in-class study comparing its operations to best practices by function or activity across industry lines.

Here's an example of an internal benchmarking study that resulted in the blending of an external benchmarking study. The internal benchmarking team performed a study of all of the activities of the Bright Light Company, a major lamp and lighting fixture manufacturer. One of its major concerns was that its customer base and market share had eroded, resulting in a large decrease in total sales and net income. As a result of these conditions, the company had been forced to cut costs drastically in all areas, including product and personnel costs. Such measures, while creating an increase in net income in the short run, had resulted in long-term deterioration of the customer base and total sales. Company management directed the internal benchmarking team to find out the causes for such loss of customer base and to recommend areas for improvement.

The company had problems with their customers ordering less from them (or not ordering at all) and more from their competitors. The study team, therefore, decided to ask present and past customers what they perceived to be the problems with Bright Light. They would also try to visit a number of competitors to determine which best practices were luring customers away. If the competitors were agreeable, they would perform a competitive external benchmarking study as well.

The study team surveyed by mail, telephone, and personal visit the company's top 20 percent of present and past customers (37 customers out of a total of 182), which resulted in over 80 percent of their total sales. They also did the same with their major competitors, which, including them, amounted to over 80 percent of total market share. The overwhelming response of these customers and competitors was that Bright Light had become non-responsive to their needs. For instance, if a customer had a firm delivery date with Bright Light, the delivery date would come and go without a word from the company. This would happen even when the customer called prior to the delivery date and was assured the merchandise would be delivered on time. Often, the product was to go into a major construction project and on-time delivery was critical. The three competitors had all installed sophisticated manufacturing control systems which allowed them to guarantee on time deliveries to all of their customers.

Other customer complaints, such as wrong products, bad products, partial shipments and so on, would go unanswered. All three competitors had successfully implemented programs of zero customer complaints. Those customers still ordering from Bright Light said that they limited their present ordering only to those items they could not get elsewhere or strictly because Bright Light's prices were lower on certain items. Most of the customers said that they would return or increase their orders with Bright Light if they could eliminate their customer service problems and meet competitor's costs. They could not live with Bright Light under present conditions—they would have to meet their competition.

The internal benchmarking team recommended that Bright Light sales management go back to their present and past customers with the offer of a customer money-back guarantee, which would be backed up by an adequately staffed customer relations department. At the same time, the company would implement manufacturing control procedures similar to their competitors so as to discipline their internal operations to ensure meeting all customer commitments (e.g., on-time deliveries) in a responsive manner. Other best practices observed at customers and competitors would also be implemented so as to bring costs and resultant prices to the same levels of their competitors.

Top management recognized that these recommendations, while they might succeed in regaining their customer base, would cost them money to put into effect. They did not believe that they were in a current position to invest this amount of money, so they decided instead to put up signs such as "the customer is our business," "we work for the customer," "the customer pays our salaries," and so on.

While the signs were done well and looked cute, after the first three months there was little improvement. In fact, nothing had changed except that customer relations personnel wrote customer phone numbers and complaints on the signs. As a result, top management asked the internal benchmarking team to implement their recommendations. Within the year, Bright Light's business had turned around. The benchmarking team was then asked to conduct a more extensive competitive external benchmarking study.

An internal benchmarking case study situation is shown in Exhibit 3.17. Please review this situation as to how it might be incorporated into an overall internal benchmarking study. Review the suggested responses to gain a greater understanding of how such situations are used to identify problem areas, causes of the problems, and the road to best practices in a program of continuous improvements.

Exhibit 3.17   Internal Benchmarking Case Study

SITUATION:

The Company decided to earmark specific customers and related sales forecasts for their product line XXX business by salesperson. For the first quarter of such directed sales planning, the results for the three sales persons were as follows:

Sales Forecast to Sales:

Salesperson	Forecast	Sales	Difference	%
Brown	2,500	4,000	1,500	160%
Gray	3,500	3,200	(300)	91%
White	4,000	3,600	(400)	90%
Totals	10,000	10,800	800	108%

140

Exhibit 3.17 *(Continued)*

Types of Sales Contacts:

Salesperson	No. of Customers	Personal Contacts	Phone Calls	Memos Sent
Brown	18	84	146	63
Gray	26	38	73	28
White	44	26	48	12

INTERNAL BENCHMARKING QUESTIONS:

As part of an internal benchmarking study of the sales function, the study team is comparing sales results to efforts.

1. What additional data should be gathered?
2. What factors should be considered for internal benchmarking?
3. Are there any conclusions or inferences that can be drawn from the above?

INTERNAL BENCHMARKING CASE STUDY SITUATION SUGGESTED RESPONSES

1. *Additional Data to Gather*

   a. *Sales Data*

      1) Seniority of salespeople
         Years with company: White 12 years, Gray eight years, Brown one year
         Age: White, 54; Gray, 46; Brown, 27
         Annual pay: White $124,000, Gray $88,000, Brown $37,000

      2) List of customers and customer statistics/history
         How long a customer
         Sales history by product with trends
         Salesperson assigned
         New customer/lost customer history

      3) Salespeople history
         Sales by customer history and trends
         Sales efforts versus results
         Forecast to actual sales history

(continues)

Exhibit 3.17 *(Continued)*

New customer history
Lost customer history

4) Sales forecast data
Sales forecast by customer/products versus actual
New customers not on forecast
Lost customers or sales on forecast
Amount of sales not materializing
Amount of sales not on forecast

b. *Contacts Data*

1) Customer survey
Satisfaction with company, products, salespeople
Relationship with assigned salesperson
If sales have decreased, why and are they buying elsewhere
What would help them to buy more
Positive and negative experiences
What do we do right—and wrong
Competitor relationships and their advantages

2) Type of contacts
Effectiveness: personal contact, phone call, memos
Relationship: contacts to salespeople (past, present, and future)
Quality of contacts by salesperson
Contact procedures by each salesperson

2. *Factors For Benchmarking*

a. Process: sales contact procedures and follow-up

b. Timeliness: how responsive is sales function to customer

c. Quality: relationship with customer, products, sales follow-up

d. Cycle: how often is customer contacted—pre-sale, during sale, and after sale

e. Numbers
Contacts/sale
Sales forecast/actual sales
Sales/sales efforts
Sales cost/gross sale/net profit on sale

3. *Conclusions/Inferences:*

a. The greater the sales contacts/customer service, the greater the possibility of increased sales.

Exhibit 3.17 *(Continued)*

---

b. Sales forecasts have little basis in reality and are not related to real sales efforts, plans, or real customer orders.

c. The more seniority of the salesperson, the fewer sales efforts and customer contacts by the sales person.

d. Sales compensation is based more on seniority than on efforts and results.

e. Sales forecasts are based on historical sales and cannot be counted on to plan production based on real customer orders.

f. There is little incentive for older sales personnel to fully service present customers and bring in new customers.

CHAPTER FOUR

External Benchmarking: Competitive, Industry, and Best-of-Class

INTRODUCTION

From an organizational standpoint, the first step in the benchmarking process is to define the company's strategic and long-term plans and directions, and its related organizational benchmarks—for the organization, divisions, departments, functions, activities, and so on. The organization should then perform an internal benchmarking study to identify its critical problem areas, identify and implement best practices, implement an organization-wide program for continuous improvements, and identify targets for a formal external benchmark study. In effect, the organization should be responsible for becoming as economical, efficient, and effective as possible on its own. At that point, if management believes that operations can be enhanced even more by formally looking at how other companies perform similar activities, then it should consider an external benchmarking study. Typically, it is at this point that management must look again at its major functions to determine the extent of its major performance gaps, compared to its competitors. In those areas where performance gaps are wide or costly (and management believes that it is advantageous and practical to close such gaps or surpass them), the economics of performing a formal external benchmarking should be considered. The study team usually identifies those areas to be considered for external benchmarking in their internal benchmarking study.

External benchmarking is normally considered a comparison to others—your competitors, your industry, or best-in-class by function. Such competitive evaluation techniques have been around for a long time, related to such things as costing and pricing. External benchmarking, however, also looks at the processes others use, together with industry and functional trends to identify opportunities for continuous improvement. It is not just a process of bringing your company up to the level of others' incompetency (although better than your own), but of identifying and implementing the best practices. Your goal should not be to compare yourself against others and then match them, but to surpass others who are after your stakeholders and profits. The goal of external benchmarking is not to blindly implement better practices others use, but to identify and implement best practices which work most efficiently for the organization. To do this effectively, the external benchmarking team must understand the workings of the organization, including such things as strategic thrusts, desired directions, organizational benchmarks, performance drivers, mental models and belief systems, internal benchmarking results, external benchmarking targets, and so on.

Based on such knowledge of the organization, the external benchmarking team decides which type of external benchmarking study to perform:

- Competitive benchmark study
- Industry benchmark study
- Best-in-class benchmark study
- Combination of the above

COMPETITIVE BENCHMARKING

Competitive benchmarking focuses its attention on direct competitors' key systems and procedures which affect competitive advantage.

It is similar to a traditional competitive evaluation analysis, but it is quite different. For instance, the study team (internal or external) might learn that the company's main competitor is manufacturing the same product in less than 10 days, while the company takes over 20 days. Such a differential in manufacturing time provides the main competitor with a competitive advantage, which it can exploit with shared customers. Knowing this, the company could get rid of its plant manager as a solution—fixing the blame, not the cause. Such a change, while constituting action, still leaves the company's processes just as inferior, and it still takes over 20 days to manufacture the product.

> ## *Systems Prevail—*
> ## *People Come and Go*

Competitive benchmarking, on the other hand, looks for reasons the work is done a certain way—not blaming the people. Its goal is to not only match your competitors, but to surpass them. External benchmarking is a continuous improvement process using present employees' knowledge, creating a learning organization, and resulting in continued innovation and change. Rather than merely replacing the plant manager (or maybe hiring additional employees), the external benchmarking study team would look for processes changes (e.g., elimination of set-ups, reduction of process time, elimination of rework and rejects, just-in-time work-in-process concepts, and so on) that not only result in manufacturing the item in 10 days, but in fewer than 10 days.

INDUSTRY BENCHMARKING

Industry benchmarking is a process used to identify industry performance and trends. While competitive benchmarking may include a limited number of competitors (three or four), industry benchmarking focuses on identifying general trends across a larger industry grouping. Industry benchmarking is a more general procedure that looks at other companies with similar interests to identify trends in customer service, products/services, personnel, processes, sales/marketing, and so on. For example, the banking industry may move from less reliance on live tellers to more reliance on automated tellers. There may even be a trend to charge for real teller services, with no charges for automated teller services. The company would appraise whether such a trend was best for it. If its emphasis is on direct customer service, this trend toward automated tellers may not be desirable. However, if its more pressing priority is to reduce costs (and maximize fees for personnel services), then use of automated tellers might be of interest. Another example of an industry trend is the movement toward internet retailing as opposed to person-to-person store retailing or catalog selling.

BEST-IN-CLASS BENCHMARKING

Best-in-class benchmarking is a process of identifying best practices across a variety of industry settings—usually by function, activity, or process. It is based on the belief that best practices can be applied across different types of industries or organizations. Many organizations are stuck in the mental model that they know their business best. For best-in-class benchmarking to be most successful, the organization must change such thinking so that it can accept that some other organization (even one outside of their industry) can do something different and better than it can. Management must seek to find the best of the best practices—no matter where it comes from—and then innovatively change the company's processes.

For example, a small manufacturer may be looking for better purchasing methods in order to reduce or eliminate the need for a central purchasing department, especially for low-cost items (where the cost of the purchase is less than the cost of processing) and repetitive purchases. As part of the company's best-in-class external benchmarking study, the study team has identified an insurance company which has successfully eliminated its central purchasing department. It accomplished this by a variety of small purchase processes such as petty cash, direct cash purchases, debit and credit cards, and so on.

It also instituted procedures whereby vendors from whom they purchase large and/or repetitive items are placed on long-term contracts which allow for releases from the contract rather than the preparation of individual purchase orders each time. In addition, it contracted with its major vendors (approximately 20 percent of all vendors who account for 80 percent of all purchases) to pay through electronic data transfer at the time of delivery. This practice also eliminated the need for the accounts payable function for these purchases. The small manufacturer must analyze the manner by which the insurance company accomplished these practices, and then determine what would be practical for its situation.

To illustrate which type of external benchmarking studies might be best in a given situation, look at the following example. William Semple was the CEO of an old family-owned regional department store chain. The company's (and most of the industry's) business philosophy was always to promote from within as a reward for loyal and faithful service. Historically, it paid its employees relatively less than other types of business in the area. However, once one of its employees reached the management ranks, the employee's compensation multiplied to far exceed the rate other companies in the area offered. The company's mental model was to reward its managers for past services and current contributions to the management team. As a long-term family business, the company had a large proportion (over 40 percent) of employees who had been in its employ for over 20 years. These employees worked for the company at area sub-standard wages as they felt "part of the family" and valued by the family itself. Due to the company's policy of rewarding past loyal service by promotion to management, over 60 percent of these employees were presently in management positions, with the others (other than part-timers) expecting to be promoted shortly as the only criteria was time with the company.

The company had always enjoyed a favorable position where it had stores. In most cases, it was the keystone store in the downtown area, emphasizing quality merchandise and service. However, in the last few years, there had been a migration from downtown shopping to suburban malls, as well as an increased emphasis on discounters.

Due to these conditions, the company was having financial difficulties for the first time in its history as sales were decreasing sharply while costs remained relatively stable.

> ## *As Belief Systems Change,*
> ## *So Do Results*

Company management was perplexed as to why its mental model of promotions of loyal employees to management positions had ceased to work effectively. It realized it had created a top-heavy management structure in numbers and costs, but the system had always worked in the past. This same philosophy of rewarding length of service had also created a management team of blind devotees to company policy and a work staff of robotic followers. As long as the company had been able to maintain its market niche, it was able to survive with this philosophy. However, with drastic changes taking place in the marketplace, it was no longer able to compete. It had succeeded in creating an organization that could only move in one direction, and unfortunately that direction had changed. From a well-meaning standpoint, it had created a work force that could neither adjust to present conditions or become effectively employable outside of the company. It decided that it needed to benchmark, not only with its competitors (who tended to use the same model), but also with others in the industry (such as discounters) and other industries which were also labor-dependent (such as restaurants, hotels and motels, banks and so on). It instituted an all-encompassing external benchmarking study (with elements of competitive, industry, and best-in-class) which resulted in changing the mental model to one of compensation for results.

ANTITRUST CONSIDERATIONS

With the conduct of an external benchmarking study encompassing competitive and/or industry analysis, there is always a consideration of antitrust litigation. The external benchmarking study consisting of competing participants can always bring forth the question of whether these competitors are colluding as to price and non-competitive practices. The external benchmarking study team needs to be careful that they stick to issues relating to best practices of operating practices and processes. If materials like pricing and collusion of the overall market arise in the external benchmarking study, the study team needs to be careful how they handle such information.

Sherman Act of 1890

Antitrust legislation started with the Sherman Act of 1890, which banned any trust or other business combination which interfered with interstate or foreign trade, monopolized, or attempted or conspired to create a monopoly. In addition, this act was also interpreted to make any fixing of prices, divisions of markets, or similar collusive activities among competitors illegal—even a crime.

Clayton Antitrust Law of 1914

This act made it illegal for corporations to group together under interlocking boards of directors. In addition, the act prohibits several unfair business practices which tend to decrease competition in certain circumstances. For example, a larger organization might buy the stock, merge, or form a joint venture with their competitors; force their customers to sign long-term exclusive agreements; or make them buy unneeded goods so they can get needed goods, in order to eliminate smaller competitors.

The Robinson-Patman Act amended the Clayton Act to outlaw price discrimination that might give favored buyers an advantage over others. The government enacted these acts to protect the free market by eliminating collusion among competing companies.

Recent Developments

Under these acts, the threat of expensive litigation and potential damages stopped communications among companies in the same industry. This may have stopped collusion, but it also may have stopped innovation. Recently, such antitrust laws have been amended to recognize the advantages of joint research and development, as exemplified by the National Cooperative Research Act of 1984—but with only limited protection. This act was partially in response to the belief that American industries were lagging behind other countries in technological developments.

Antitrust and Benchmarking

The issue in benchmarking is really whether gaining knowledge about competitive practices is the same as collusion among competitors. Antitrust laws as mentioned above are concerned with exchanges of information which lead to price fixing or limitations on competition. Such laws should not be concerned with information exchange between competitors which allows for more vigorous competition—the results of benchmarking studies. The study team must ensure that this is the case.

If benchmarking studies are conducted correctly, they shouldn't impinge upon the antitrust laws. If the benchmarking study focuses on improving the processes by which products and services are produced, distributed, or serviced; antitrust laws shouldn't apply. The benchmarking study focus is not on pricing or market share, but on determining best practices. Unless change or continuous improvement is forbidden by antitrust laws; benchmarking for best practices should be free from antitrust legislation.

The government has not specifically addressed benchmarking *per se*, but most legal experts seem to feel that as long as benchmarking studies don't address price information or future plans, they are probably safe from antitrust legislation. As long as the study focuses on processes rather than competitive prices, antitrust laws do not apply. When a benchmarking study is conducted properly, it should be far removed from the concerns of antitrust legislation.

Although there are no known cases filed as a result of benchmarking studies, there have been several indications by the federal government that legitimize such sharing of process data.

- Malcolm Baldridge National Quality Award (Public Law 100-107) requires for more than half its points the comparison of performance to outside entities. In effect, the government has become a proponent of benchmarking.
- The federal government uses benchmarking as an analytical tool in a number of military departments and other agencies.
- As of this date, the federal government has not initiated any enforcement actions against benchmarking activities.

Antitrust issues are a complex area and should be reviewed by a legal advisor. If the study team believes the risks of antitrust legislation to be too great, they may want to consider benchmarking with companies who are not their direct competitors or who are outside of their industry. The benchmarking team can make direct comparisons of various functions and activities such as management and administration, accounting and finance, sales and marketing, and so on. In addition, the study team can limit their benchmarking activities to internal operational reviews within their own organization where such risk of antitrust legislation ceases to exist.

QUANTITATIVE AND QUALITATIVE BENCHMARKS

Whichever type of external benchmarking study the company decides to conduct, company management and study team members should be aware of some typical external benchmarking targets. Some of these benchmark targets may have been identified by the organization and/or study team as a result of the internal benchmarking study. Other benchmark targets may be identified through preparation for the external benchmarking study. Still others may not be identified until the external benchmarking study is in process. Keep in mind that the organization may perform an internal benchmarking study only, an external benchmarking study only, or both an internal and external benchmarking study. In any case, such external benchmarking targets should be identified at the beginning of the study, and then enhanced during the study, by the external benchmarking team and others within the company.

Exhibit 4.1 provides a list of some quantitative benchmarks and exhibit 4.2 provides a list of some qualitative benchmarks. These lists can be used to identify those benchmarks which should be included in the company's external benchmarking study. These lists can also be starting points, where the study team may wish to add, change, or delete items for inclusion in their study.

EXHIBIT 4.1   Quantitative External Benchmarks

Productivity

- Productivity—number of items produced
- Number of employees
- Amount of time
- Cost per good unit produced
- Total productivity versus total cost
- Items or transactions processed by employee
- Orders shipped per hour by employee
- Increase or decrease in inventory by item
- Inventory turnover ratios
- Comparisons: automated, semi-automated, manual processes
- Reduction or elimination of processing time: set-ups, processing, put away
- Actual results compared to schedules
- Timeliness—vendors, into production, work in process, shipment and deliveries
- Currentness—elimination of backlog, processing up to date

Quality

- Number of good pieces
- Amount of scrap
- Amount and cost of rework
- Amount and cost of quality inspection
- Receiving vendor rejects
- Number of customer returns
- Number of customer complaints
- Warranty claims
- Returns and allowances
- Good units produced
- Amount of material in to produce a given quantity

EXHIBIT 4.1   *(Continued)*

- Parts availability
- On-time deliveries
- Sales forecast accuracy

Timeliness

- On-time deliveries
- Design time—customer to finished design
- Production lead time
- Purchasing to vendor delivery time
- Shipping time
- Number of late orders
- Number of late deliveries
- Number of back orders
- Set-ups—number and time
- Inspections—number and time
- Non-productive time
- Order processing time

Accounting

- Number of items—invoices, payments, payroll time cards
- Number of bills at time of shipment
- Number of payments at terms time
- Accuracy of processing
- Number of accounts payable debits
- Number of accounts receivable credits
- Employee productivity statistics
- Timeliness and accuracy of reporting

Exhibit 4.2   Qualitative External Benchmarks

Products or Services

- Number of products and/or services
- Number of activities or moves
- Number of total parts and/or activities
- Number of standard items
- Number of options offered
- Specialty items offered

(continues)

Exhibit 4.2 *(Continued)*

- Number of products or services produced—by unit, equipment, location
- Number of stockouts or inability to provide product or service
- Amount of delays or time promised changes
- Acceptability of each product or service
- Sales trends of each product or service
- Product reorders
- Product returns
- After sale service and costs
- New products or services
- Product enhancements
- Discontinued products or services and reasons why

Facilities/Capacity

- Number of work units
- Number of personnel
- Number and location of bottlenecks
- Number of changes
- Amount of preventive maintenance
- Demand fluctuation
- Number of quality control inspections
- Conditions over and under capacity
- Smoothness of work flow
- Ability to schedule: actual versus schedule
- Conditions: clean and organized versus cluttered
- Type and condition of equipment
- Responsibility for work areas
- Direct receipt of raw materials into production
- Control over work in process
- Direct customer shipment from production

Customer Satisfaction

- Amount of repeat business
- Satisfaction
- Actual performance versus promises
- Referrals to others
- Perceptions—quality, price, ease of use, features
- Trends in existing customer sales

Exhibit 4.2 *(Continued)*

- Number of new customers and retention rates
- Positive comments or appraisals
- Timeliness: on time deliveries
- Positive comments
- Amount of increased business
- Sales trends by major customer

Marketing/Sales

- Number of salespeople
- Amount of marketing effort
- Increases in sales—number, profits, by customer, by salesperson
- Customer support
- Amount of flexibility
- Product success rates
- Sales to existing customers
- Number and sales to new customers
- Sales forecasts—accuracy and ratio to real customer orders
- Marketing/sales costs to total sales
- Sales of right items to right customers at the right time

Processing

- Time to process an order
- Number of contacts per order filled
- Number of errors
- Time to get order into production
- Time to process shipping
- Time to process billing
- Collection statistics
- Number of orders in backlog
- Amount of backlog never realized

CHOOSING A BENCHMARKING APPROACH

We have discussed internal benchmarking as a process whereby you can compare and standardize internal operations as to best practices as well as identify opportunities for positive improvements and areas for external benchmarking. Those areas identified for external benchmarking encompass those functions and activities that management believes can be substantially improved through comparison to other organizations. The expected results must compensate the effort and cost of performing the external benchmarking study. Such external benchmarking techniques can measure and compare your company's performance in all areas of operations, such as manufacturing or the providing of services, financial and accounting, and support services such as computer processing, sales and marketing, personnel, customer service, and so on. These operating practices of the company can be compared to competitors (e.g., competitive analysis), industry (e.g., industry trends), and across functional or activity areas (e.g., best-in-class for purchasing practices).

Internal benchmarking and its related operational reviews can be a tool for continuous company improvement (sometimes an end in itself) and/or the initial movement toward a more encompassing external benchmarking study. Competitive benchmarking helps to identify and prioritize those critical areas of the company to be subjected to more intense review and improvement efforts. Industry benchmarking helps to identify trends and how the company can use these trends best. Best-in-class benchmarking targets the identification of best practices across specific functional areas with companies in other industries and settings. The objective is to match the processes performed (e.g., handling manufacturing set-ups), not the type or structure of the companies involved.

The objective of all of these benchmarking procedures is not to score your company against others, but to use your findings as an organizational learning tool—to support continual growth, learning, and improvement. Benchmarking provides targets as part of strategic, long-term, short-term, and detail planning. It takes into account the mental models, belief systems, performance drivers, and measures of the various organizations included in the external benchmarking study.

In choosing the benchmarking approach (competitive, industry, or best-in-class) that is best for the company's situation, there are various factors. If the main thrust of the company is to meet and beat the competition, then competitive benchmarking may be the best course. If the company desires to be the best in the industry, then industry benchmarking could be the most useful. If the company focuses on its processes and desires to perform each of their functions and activities in the best manner possible, then best-in-class benchmarking would be most effective. The company could also perform its external benchmarking study to include aspects of all three types of benchmarking. That is, competitive benchmarking for customer service, industry benchmarking for product standardization, and best-in-class benchmarking for the shipping function.

PERFORMANCE DRIVERS

Benchmarking techniques are now identified with the development of internal and external scorecards which allow others to review comparable performance to the leaders of best practices. Sometimes the organization blindly follows such best practices, with little regard to the applicability of the practice to the specifics of the situation. Benchmarking, however, is more concerned with continuous and future improvement. It focuses on future operating and performance goals—setting the stage for strategic and short-term planning directed toward achievement of such goals. As part of the benchmarking process, performance drivers and constraints are identified—such as outmoded mental models, management assumptions, and belief systems. By reducing or eliminating these barriers, internal improvements become more possible—leading the way toward internal best practices.

A performance driver is an underlying characteristic or factor of the company or its environment that determines the amount and type of activities performed to meet stakeholder demands. Performance drivers can be embedded in the organizational environment (e.g., conservative banking and informal technology companies), part of the organizational culture (e.g., dress code and expected behavior), company or industry tradition (e.g., paperwork and excessive controls), or performance-related (e.g., customer complaint responses and sales at all costs). Performance drivers provide the answer to "why things are done in that manner?" in the benchmarking process. Part of the benchmarking team's organizational analysis must encompass the unique idiosyncrasies of the company and management preferences, locational constraints, and other non-negotiable areas such as work schedules, company policies, organizational hierarchies, budget systems and procedures, hiring and promotion criteria, and so on.

It is important for the external benchmarking team to identify its company's performance drivers as well as those of other companies included in the benchmarking study. Often, it is the performance drivers of the various organizations included in the external benchmarking study which allow for one company to achieve a best practice with corresponding positive results, while another company using the same practice achieves negative results. For example, one company using the practice of employee self-responsibility has been able to achieve productivity improvements of over 60%, while another company who has not relaxed its need to closely control all employees has seen productivity drop by over 20 percent. The best practice may indeed be the most economical, efficient, and effective practice available. However, without addressing the necessary changes in the organization's performance drivers, it may become even worse than the ineffective present practice. It is not only necessary to identify a best practice, but it is also necessary to know how to successfully implement such a best practice within the structure of the organization.

Some examples of such organizational performance drivers are shown in Exhibit 4.3.

Exhibit 4.3   Organizational Performance Drivers

Organizational Environment

- Company policies (e.g., in to work and out of work at specified times)
- Management and employee skills and abilities (e.g., cooperative versus competitive)
- Market constraints (e.g., price, quality)

Exhibit 4.3   *(Continued)*

- Product constraints (e.g., labor or material intensive)
- Technology (e.g., high, low, innovative)
- Organizational structure (e.g., over-controlling hierarchy versus loosely controlled)
- Management philosophy (e.g., short-term sales versus long term growth)

Organizational Culture

- Working atmosphere (e.g., comfortable socialization versus oppressive and controlling)
- Type of structure (e.g., unwieldy hierarchy versus integrated and working together)
- Single product versus diversified (e.g., bicycles versus auto parts and food products)
- Locations and number of facilities (e.g., headquarters and branches versus one central location)
- Upward/downward/horizontal communication patterns (e.g., free flowing communication patterns versus controlled communication)
- Control elements (e.g., strong central control versus properly delegated authority)
- Job and behavioral expectations (e.g., do the job exactly as you are told versus effective, self-motivated, disciplined behavior and self-responsibility)
- Embedded value system (e.g., quality is important versus ship in any condition)
- Evaluation and reward systems (e.g., salary increase and promotions based on seniority versus rewards based on results)

Performance-Related

- Hiring, orientation, training, evaluation, and promotion practices and criteria (e.g., automatic based on length of service versus objective appraisal)
- Turnover or lack thereof (e.g., employees coming and going versus long-term employees staying where compensation compares with results)
- Delegation of authority and responsibilities (e.g., effective delegation of authority down to the lowest levels possible relative to responsibilities versus authority controlled at the top of the organization)

(continues)

Exhibit 4.3   *(Continued)*

- Unwieldy organizational hierarchy (e.g., excessive layers of reporting relationship versus self-responsibility in a coaching and facilitative environment)
- Overlaps of responsibility and job functions (e.g., clear definitions versus duplications and redundancies)
- Emphasis on economy, efficiency, and effectiveness (e.g., program of continuous improvements in a learning organization versus empire building)
- Quality and use of information systems (e.g., effectively used for management decisions versus overload of data)

The following is an example of how performance drivers affect the operation of an organization. Randy Nelson built his plumbing fixtures and supplies business through hard work and long hours. He and his wife Mandy started the business over twenty years ago. The business started as a small mom and pop type business selling their products to individual small business plumbers and do-it-yourself homeowners. The business was located in a town of about 80,000 in population, over 100 miles from a large urban area of over one million in population. As the large urban area deteriorated over the years, people began to move toward Randy's town until at this point it was a growth area of over 250,000 people. Randy's company was the primary supplier for almost all of the major building developers and contractors in the area. His business had grown far beyond expectations and he was now basically a "non-working" President of a corporate empire with six retail locations and three supply depots with over 60 employees.

Randy established his organization structure to fit his easygoing, friendly personality, which also reflected the way he treated employees and customers. This easy-going friendly manner for doing business became the primary performance driver for the company. Based on this manner, Randy had effectively delegated authority and responsibility to his employees, and each of the company's locations ran autonomously as distinct profit centers. The achievement of expectations and results was rewarded objectively and each employee was treated as an entrepreneur—basically in business for him or herself. Randy developed simple systems which provided him with the key information he needed to oversee and manage effectively without putting in long hours.

Randy's son Sandy had worked in the business since he was fourteen years old. Randy expressed a number of times that Sandy should have it easier than he and Mandy did. Sandy received his bachelors and masters degrees in business—a dream that Randy never imagined would happen. When Sandy graduated as an MBA, Randy made him President of the company. Randy became Chairman of the Board and hoped that Sandy would continue to run the company in the same easy-going, friendly manner as he had done.

> ### The Best System Is the Simple System— and the One That Works

Sandy wanted to apply what he had learned at MBA school, using the company as his case study. The first thing Sandy did was to change reporting relationships and existing performance drivers, so that each location and individual employee reported directly to him. He then proceeded to change the simple and basic reporting system so that he could have all of the detail operating data for his analysis. Based on this data, Sandy would call or visit those individuals who might be screwing up. He changed the basic performance drivers of the organization and created an organizational reign of terror. All of the key employees who had been responsible for the success of the company threatened to quit. Randy had to come back and help Sandy unlearn what he had been taught in MBA school.

CONCLUSION

Once the organization has decided to embark on an external benchmarking study, it needs to decide which areas to include in the study. Should the company have proceeded through the benchmarking process as discussed previously, it would have defined its reason for existing, what businesses it is in and not in, its strategic plans and thrusts; organizational, departmental, functional, and activity benchmarks; and so on. It would also have conducted an internal benchmarking study enabling it to implement best practices in all of its major operating areas. As a result of the internal benchmarking study, areas were identified that could be further improved by comparing such activities to other organizations. It is these areas that are included in the organization's external benchmarking study.

The organization needs to decide which type of external benchmarking study best fits its needs—competitive, industry, best-in-class, or a combination. In considering such an external benchmarking study, the organization must consider which external benchmarking targets to include. This requires a thorough analysis and knowledge of the company's operations and where they see critical benchmarking performance gaps and opportunities for best practice improvements. Based on expected external benchmarking results, the organization is then in a position to develop their benchmarking approach. This could include the attributes of desirable benchmarking partners, which benchmarking targets to include in the study, the approach to be taken, and so on. The organization also needs to be thoroughly knowledgeable as to those internal performance drivers that enhance the company's ability to perform and produce results and those that inhibit positive progress.

The next chapter will discuss the external benchmarking process, how to implement successful external benchmarking procedures, and how to achieve maximum results from such a study.

CHAPTER FIVE

External Benchmarking Process

INTRODUCTION

The first step in preparing for the external benchmarking study is to determine which areas to include in the study. These areas have been defined as a result of an internal benchmarking study or through proper analysis of the organization's functions as to where critical performance gaps exist. It is extremely important to accurately define those critical areas to be included in the external benchmarking so that study time is used most expeditiously and time is not wasted on less significant areas.

It is also extremely important to select the correct members of the external benchmarking team—both other organization participants as well as individual members of the benchmarking team. It is then critical that the team conducts the external benchmarking study correctly and properly. As such an external benchmarking study may take considerable time and expense, it is important that such resources are used effectively to produce maximum results for the organization.

This chapter discusses some recommended techniques and procedures for conducting an effective external benchmarking study. Such techniques must be tailored to the specific requirements of the organization conducting the study. Although an organization may not desire to conduct ongoing external benchmarking studies, the organization must see the study as part of their program for continuous improvements. The external benchmarking process doesn't stop at the end of the study, but continues on throughout the life of the organization. There are many other sources for benchmark comparisons other than continual formal studies. Such comparisons need to become an integral part of the organization's management and operations processes. Benchmarking, identification, and implementation of best practices, and conducting of an ongoing program of continuous improvements becomes the responsibility of each and every employee.

THE BENCHMARKING TEAM

An external benchmarking study (as well as an internal benchmarking study) can consume a considerable amount of personnel time and effort. While there are procedures for continual review of operations, the formal benchmarking study is not normally performed on a frequent repetitive basis. It is more of a one-time study, with possible follow-up in the future. It is, therefore, extremely important that the study team consists of the most appropriate individuals. The study results will typically be in direct proportion to the qualities, skills, and attributes of the members of the study team.

Most important for a benchmarking study, those employees who are responsible for the implementation of recommended best practice changes based on the results of the benchmarking study, will be most successful if they are part of the study team. Another consideration for choosing members of the study team is that different individuals possess different perspectives, special skills or abilities, a variety of business-related experiences and contacts, special knowledge, and so on. It is extremely important to choose team members so that these differing attributes work best together.

The benchmarking team can consist entirely of individuals employed by the organization (typically an internal benchmarking team), or it may consist of personnel from the host organization as well as employees of other study participant companies (typically an external benchmarking team). In either case, outsiders such as consultants, experts, and specialists can join the team when appropriate. Including team members who work in the areas under consideration is helpful in identifying present and possible best practices as well as in advocating implementation of recommended best practice changes.

Individuals selected for the team from outside of the areas under study (within or outside of the host company) are usually chosen for their specific knowledge, skills, abilities, and special expertise. In addition, they should represent their work area or organization. The benchmarking team is typically brought together for this sole purpose. Members of the team may be assigned full-time to the study or may continue to have work responsibilities. Often, once the benchmarking study is complete, the benchmarking team is disbanded. Members of the team may also assist in the implementation of recommended best practice changes.

Members of the benchmarking team can work effectively with individuals working in the areas under study to assist them in looking at their present practices to question the necessity of procedures and develop better ways to accomplish results. In this manner, these employees are already sold on recommended best practices and will advocate for change. These employees will help to ease the transition from present practices to best practices. The previous team members can also assist these work areas in developing the residual capability for implementing an effective program for continuous improvements after the initial study is completed.

Criteria for individuals for selection to the benchmarking team could include the following:

- Special skills and abilities
- Knowledge of the areas included in the study
- Mutual respect—within the team and with the organizations participating in the study
- Communication skills—both oral and written
- Team orientation—ability to work together as team players
- Analytical ability—to analyze a situation, identify the problem, causes, and recommend corrective actions

- Motivation to learn—desire to expand learning and use it for effective problem solving
- Management skills—project management, working with diverse groups, and a multifunctional environment

In developing the benchmark team, it is also important to consider the aspect of group (and team) dynamics—that is the manner in which the team must work together. There should be a project manager or team leader. This can be one individual or the team can share project management responsibilities. Such sharing is usually effective where a number of organizations or functions are included in the study, such as a competitive external benchmarking study. Through the sharing of project management, control by one individual or organization is minimized, the results tend to be shared more effectively, and results are accepted more readily. Other special team assignments or responsibilities that might be considered include project facilitation for such things as coordination, scheduling, and progress meetings; operational reviewers; interviewers; data collection tool developers; data analyzers; best practice developers and implementers; oral reporting presenters; report writers, and so on.

There are no hard and fast rules as to the size and composition of the benchmarking team. It will vary based on the needs of the internal or external benchmarking study. Normally, a team of less than ten individuals works best—the smaller the better. Should the benchmarking team become too large for the situation, it may become ineffective. Team infighting and resultant indecisiveness may result, decreasing the quality of the benchmarking study results. In such situations, an outside consultant or study adviser can work effectively to ensure that each individual team member participates effectively and on schedule, and that the team achieves the appropriate results.

CHOOSING BENCHMARKING STUDY PARTICIPANTS

Once the type of external benchmarking study (competitive, industry, best-in-class, or combination) and the benchmarking team (company representatives) have been chosen, the company then needs to decide which other organizations to include in the study. There are many factors that contribute to an appropriate participant for the benchmarking study. Some of these include:

- Type of business—how similar to the host company?
- Size of business—gross sales, net income, number of employees, number of locations
- Type of ownership—public corporation, private corporation, closely held, family, and so on
- Organizational structure—single business, multibusinesses, strict hierarchical, loosely organized
- Geography—local, regional, national, international
- Product mix—single product, multiproduct lines, low-mid-high end, diversified
- Market share—by product line and percentage
- Distribution methods—direct, wholesale, mail order, internet

Each potential participant should be analyzed based on the above attributes and others to determine which organizations would make the best match for the planned benchmarking study. Potential benchmarking study participants can be evaluated on whatever criteria that the study team considers to be most appropriate.

The study team can consult with a number of different parties to identify which companies would make appropriate benchmarking partners, such as:

- Vendors
- Customers
- Outside consultants
- Banks and financial institutions
- Employees—management and operations personnel
- Members of the study team
- Professional associations
- Benchmarking groups

Once the potential benchmarking study participants have been identified, host company personnel (usually a member of the study team or an employee who has a significant contact) should contact the organization to determine whether it is interested in being a participant in the planned benchmarking study. The host company should not force themselves on the potential participant. If there is no willingness on the company's part to participate, they will probably not be a willing and cooperative participant. After the study participants have been selected, each should contribute to the study—personnel and time.

PARTICIPATION AGREEMENT

Some organizations feel more comfortable as part of an external benchmarking study—either as the prime or host study conductor, or as one of the study participants—to have the agreement between all participants in writing. Such a written agreement not only formalizes (as a form of contract) the benchmarking study relationship, but also clarifies such things as:

- Scope of areas to be benchmarked (e.g., entire organization, specific location(s), department, functions, or activities)
- Depth of the review in each area (e.g., questionnaire only, on-site general review, or on-site detailed operations review)
- Decision-making mechanism (e.g., organizationally, individuals)
- Resources committed to the project (e.g., individuals—who and amount of time, equipment, computer processing, and so on)
- Each party's expectations (e.g., findings, conclusions, recommendations, reporting, implementation)
- Study results—how reported, confidentiality, distribution
- Project costs—who pays and for what, in-kind contributions

The participation agreement should be documented and signed by all study participants prior to the start of the benchmarking study. Having such a participant agreement is particularly significant when you are benchmarking:

- Competitors
- Highly confidential functions or activities
- Highly technical or costly areas
- To ultimately publish study results

A sample external benchmarking study participation agreement is shown in Exhibit 5.1. Note that this sample agreement should be individualized to the external benchmarking team's specific circumstances, legal requirements, and study purposes.

Exhibit 5.1 Sample External Benchmarking Participation Agreement

PARTICIPANTS:	STUDY AREAS:
Our Company, Rob Reider	Purchasing
ABC Company, Joe Smith	Receiving
DEF Company, Carol Olson	Accounts Payable
GHI Company, Susan Booth	
JKL Company, David Luce	

This agreement is made between the above mentioned parties and specifies the responsibilities of each participant in the external benchmarking study to be undertaken.

STUDY COORDINATOR

Rob Reider, representing Our Company, in the role of study coordinator, will lead an external benchmarking study in which the above mentioned companies have agreed to participate and benefit from its findings.

WORK STEPS AND RESPONSIBILITIES

Our Company will be responsible for the conduct of the benchmarking study in accordance with the "Benchmarking Code of Conduct" and

(continues)

Exhibit 5.1 *(Continued)*

benchmarking methods in use at Our Company. The major work steps and responsibilities in the conducting of the benchmark study are as follows:

- All parties are to research each subject area in support of this project. Such research could include review and analysis of technical journals and other magazine articles, public statistics, public and private databases, newspapers, consultants, and so on.
- Mr. Rob Reider, as benchmarking study leader, will be responsible for the following:
  - Format and content of questionnaires
  - Contact with and between other study participant coordinators
  - Time lines and due dates
  - Methodology for screening erroneous data
  - Formats for reporting
- Benchmarking team members' responsibilities:
  - Solicit input from the study participants, prepare questionnaires, flow charts, and other study methodologies
  - Hold orientation sessions for filling out surveys, questionnaires, and the like
  - Distribute questionnaire and survey materials
  - Monitor the data collection efforts
  - Clarify questions, definitions, and methods
  - Design and implement a data system for tabulating and analyzing survey and questionnaire responses
  - Participate in on-site reviews with each study participant (This may be a general or detail review based on responses.)
  - Identify best practices through effective analysis
  - Organize and conduct on-site follow-up visits with those study participants exhibiting best practices
  - Develop and conduct workshop sessions to summarize and present study findings, conclusions, and recommendations to all study participants
  - Document findings, conclusions, and recommendations in a formal written report for distribution to all participants (The report will maintain strict confidentiality of each study participant unless given permission to do otherwise.)

Exhibit 5.1 *(Continued)*

STUDY COMPLETION

The external benchmarking study will be considered complete when:

- All study work steps have been completed.
- Study findings and summary workshops have been held.
- Final report is written and delivered to all participants.

    Note: Participants will not have the right to publish and discuss the results of the study except with the approval of each member of the study.

EXPECTATIONS OF STUDY PARTICIPANTS

Each study participant is expected to:

- Develop and provide benchmarking data on a timely and accurate basis
- Coordinate on-site visit(s) to their facilities by the benchmarking team
- Attend benchmarking study meetings—entrance, progress/status, and final meetings
- Inform senior management of benchmarking study progress
- Provide access to benchmarking team personnel to collect study data

ACCESS AND USE OF CONFIDENTIAL INFORMATION

During the course of this study, participants will have access to confidential information of participating companies. Such confidential information is to be used by the benchmarking team only in conjunction with this agreement and for no other purpose without the consent of all study participants. No benchmarking team member shall disclose to any third party such confidential information unless it has obtained written permission to do so from all participating parties.

SHARE OF STUDY COSTS

Each study participant agrees to share equally the benchmarking study costs for such out-of-pocket items as food, lodging, meeting rooms, outside consultants, outsider services, and the like.

(continues)

Exhibit 5.1 *(Continued)*

AGREED:

Our Company: _____ Date: _____

ABC Company: _____ Date: _____

DEF Company: _____ Date: _____

GHI Company: _____ Date: _____

JKL Company: _____ Date: _____

THE STRATEGIC PLANNING INSTITUTE COUNCIL ON BENCHMARKING AND THE BENCHMARKING CODE OF CONDUCT

The Strategic Planning Institute (SPI) located in Cambridge, Massachusetts has organized a Council on Benchmarking. The SPI Council on Benchmarking provides a forum where people who coordinate benchmarking programs in their companies can meet and share information. Members of the council are primarily large, diversified corporations, most of them global in scope. Although from different industries, they have a common interest in benchmarking, and most have experience in the process. Membership is open to organizations who are committed to using benchmarking to improve the effectiveness and efficiency of their operations.

The SPI Council on Benchmarking defines benchmarking as "a systematic process for measuring products, services, and practices against external partners to achieve improved performance." They further state that benchmarking is a general purpose technique for improving business operation by learning from the experience of others.

The SPI Council on Benchmarking holds periodic meetings for members to share their own experiences. As an example, at one of their roundtable sessions, members of the SPI Council on Benchmarking were asked to use their project experience to develop a list of practices that help assure implementation of benchmarking findings. This was in response to the statement that it is easier to come up with benchmarking findings than it is to implement them. However, the council agreed, without implementation, there will be no substantive improvements. Here are the lists they developed:

Define What to Benchmark and Develop the Project Scope

- Educate executives on benchmarking including the time commitment and secure their commitment to change
- Consider the culture of the organization relative to project scope (e.g., How open is the organization to change?)
- Consider the size and specificity of the project; match scope of project with resources
- Understand customer requirements
- Ensure that all players are involved
- Link the benchmarking initiative to strategic objectives
- Develop a continuous communication plan
- Review risks (e.g., Will the team's champion change? Is the organization in the process of a merger? Is a reorganization in process?)
- Consider financial constraints—does the organization have funding to implement potential findings? Consider potential payback.

Document the Current Process

- Identify gaps and opportunities (e.g., metrics, dollars)
- Affirm commitment to change (implementation) on the part of the sponsor, the organization, affected customers, and team members
- Focus secondary research on implementation issues
- Review team participants based on implementation issues
- Identify implementation obstacles or potential problems from the process map
- Identify and educate change agents

Conduct Secondary Research and Select Partners

- Define scope of implementation (internal, international, USA)
- Gather as much information as possible about partners' current situation
- Communicate implications of budget and time constraints (e.g., partners chosen by proximity, limited research)
- Communicate selection criteria to champion/sponsor
- Consider credibility (internal image of potential partners)— credibility should represent 15–20 percent of selection weight

Analyze and Tailor Findings to Current Culture

- Communicate findings to:
  - ❑ Process owners
  - ❑ Employees impacted by change
  - ❑ Management
- Link findings to performance indicators
- Link findings to strategic direction
- Define WIIFM—"What's In It For Me?"
- Publicize success/learnings
- Recognize benchmarking team

As benchmarking typically involves cooperation between companies, the SPI Council on Benchmarking has developed a number of tools and statements which have been generally accepted by those involved in conducting external benchmarking studies. Their Benchmarking Code of Conduct outlines the ground rules that protect the intellectual property and legal interests of the parties. They are broken down into seven principles:

1. **Legality.** Avoid discussions or actions that could imply an interest in restraint of trade: market or customer allocation schemes, price fixing, dealing arrangements, bid rigging, bribery, or misappropriation.

2. **Exchange.** Be willing to provide the same level of information you request.
3. **Confidentiality.** Benchmarking interchange should be treated as confidential to the individuals or organizations involved.
4. **Use.** Use information obtained through benchmarking partnering for improvement of operations within the partnering companies themselves. External use requires permission of that partner.
5. **First Party Contact.** Initiate contacts, when possible, through a benchmarking contact designated by the partner company.
6. **Third Party Contact.** Obtain permission from an individual before providing their name in response to a contact request.
7. **Preparation.** Demonstrate efficiency and effectiveness in the benchmarking process with adequate preparation at each process step, particularly at the initial partnering contact.

Other tools offered by the SPI Council on Benchmarking include:

- Benchmarking Etiquette and Ethics, which provide the guidelines to be applied to partners in a benchmarking study.
- The Benchmarking Exchange Protocol, which outlines principles of professional behavior that insure the productive exchange of information.
- Frequently Asked Questions About Benchmarking.

The above materials with regard to the SPI Council on Benchmarking are available on their web site www.thespinet.org.

BENCHMARKING IMPLEMENTATION SCHEDULE

A successful external benchmarking study starts with senior management commitment, the identification of those critical operational areas to be included in the study, and then follows an organized set of work steps or procedures, such as the following five steps:

Step 1. Identification, Assignment, and Orientation of Benchmarking Team

- Identification of members of the external benchmarking team within the company, from other company study participants, outsiders (e.g., consultants, functional specialists)
- Assignment of roles—responsibilities, study management, reporting relationships
- Orientation and training—purpose of study, understanding of study participants, knowledge of functional areas, and so on

Step 2. Internal Company Data Gathering And Analysis

- Identify critical area(s) for review—company and other study participants
- Develop the benchmarking team (insiders and outsiders)
- Perform an internal operational review of present systems and procedures
- Identify performance drivers and constraints—for the companies and the functional areas or activities under review
- Identify desired internal practices (best practices or desired performance levels) using criteria of best practices or the collection of existing practices across the company.
- Identify performance gaps or areas where existing practices are unsatisfactory
- Correct the areas for immediate improvement
- Document areas for short-term, mid-term, and long-term improvements and those areas for further study or external benchmarking

Step 3. External Data Gathering

- Develop the external benchmarking approach, study objectives, and plan for conducting the study
- Perform necessary research—literature, periodicals, journals, databases, and so on

- Identify external benchmarking participants (competitors, industry, or best in class), organizations, and people
- Develop participant agreement—establish conditions for all parties in the study and have each party sign off on the agreement
- Develop an external benchmarking study questionnaire, interview documents, and related data collection tools
- Perform questionnaire procedures with timely completion— conduct site visits, interviews, and operational reviews; and other data collection procedures
- Review collected data and perform follow-up if necessary to ensure accuracy and validity of data

Step 4. Analysis of Benchmarking Information

- Compare obtained benchmark data of others to company performance levels—present and desired
- Identify similarities and differences—your company and benchmark participants
- Classify and analyze quantitative collected data—by participant, by function, and by activity—and compare to your company
- Analyze qualitative data (e.g., questionnaire and interview comments) and identify unique and innovative approaches
- Confirm data and comments—if necessary—by telephone or additional site visit
- Re-analyze data results based on qualitative information, which may require follow-up or clarification
- Develop recommendations (model) for best practice for area detailing implementation procedures and expected benefits and make sure that recommendations are practical and reasonable for your company
- Communicate study results (and best practices) to company and benchmark study participants. Maintain confidentiality as stated by all participants.

Step 5. Implementing Your Recommendations

- Develop an implementation team (which could include study personnel as well as others)
- Identify tasks to improve internal operations—immediate, short-term, long-term, and further study
- Prioritize performance gaps based on company plans, strategies, stakeholder demands, and costs versus benefits
- Implement benchmarking recommendations, working with the personnel in the area and others as necessary
- Develop measures for improvement to reinforce the change process and motivate acceptance
- Establish ongoing measurement techniques to show improvements or failures
- Develop effective communication systems of results, with reporting mechanism and responsibility for follow-up
- Implement procedures to work with personnel in each area to establish plan for achieving best practice and create ongoing learning environment
- Educate operations personnel in operational review and benchmarking techniques so that residual capability for future improvements remains in existence
- Develop system of continuous improvements within the organization and the functional areas
- Benchmark again (continuous basis) to maintain best practices
- Develop ongoing organization-wide communication system so that benchmarking system perpetuates itself
- Establish follow-up mechanism of periodic review
- Implement ongoing reporting or scorecard system to maintain improvements

To effectively implement recommendations generated from an external benchmarking study, there needs to be consistent agreement from all levels of the organization—starting at the top and going down to those operations personnel who must work with the recommended change. As an example, Ralph worked in a very autocratic, oppressive organization, with a large, unwieldy, hierarchical organization structure containing many layers of supervision and management. Each succeeding layer of management exerted its power and control over those levels of the organization reporting to it. The organizational atmosphere could be best described as fearful and threatening, with most employees afraid to make a move on their own without proper management approval. The organization had been this way for many years, assuming the belief system of its founder J. Rupert Johnson, a very strict and controlling individual. Each succeeding CEO was chosen for the same traits and maintained the organization in this form.

The company tried all of the available quick fixes over the years such as participative management, management by objectives, zero-based budgeting, team building, total quality management, re-engineering, re-structuring, and so on. There was always a number of different consulting firms working with them on various corrective measures. However, nothing seemed to change since nothing ever changed at the top. Ralph had gone through all of the training programs and understood the basic principles of all the proposed management systems changes. However, as a non-manager, he was not presently in a position to implement any of these systems.

> ## *There Is No Single Panacea,*
> ## *But a Combination*

Ralph was eventually promoted to manager of his department. He would finally have his opportunity to put into place all of the things he had learned in the various training programs over the years. The first thing Ralph did was to create problem-solving groups within his department and establish the concept of participative management. The work group came up with a number of innovative ways to do things better, more efficiently, and at less cost. Ralph gave them the go-ahead without approval from his boss as he believed he had full authority to run his own department. Within the first two weeks of implementing the new systems, one of the new ideas hit a snag which resulted in backing up sales orders. He and his employees were already working on correcting the situation, when his boss harassed him over the slippage with the clear message that this was never to happen again. The next day Ralph changed everything back to the way it was before, with all the work to go through him for approval.

The company decided to conduct an external benchmarking study to determine where they were deficient as to best practices. Ralph was assigned as a member of the study team. He insisted that top management define their organizational benchmarks, belief systems, basic principles of doing business, performance drivers, and so on. The results of the study supported many of the changes that Ralph had previously initiated. Now, with the study supporting him and management's stated desires, he (and the company) had little trouble or resistance in implementing best practices and a program of continuous improvements.

DATA COLLECTION PROCEDURES

The benefits of the external benchmarking process are maximized by the amount and accuracy of objective data collected from a variety of sources. As part of the benchmarking study, the study team must review and analyze as many publications relating to competition, industry, and function as possible. These publications can be books, magazines, trade journals, professional associations materials, databases (Internet, world wide web, CD-ROM), and so on. In addition, study team members must talk to internal and external personnel and experts, professional association staff, professional contacts (vendors, customers, competitors, non-competitors, consultants, etc.), and other relevant individuals and groups.

A summary of sources for such data collection as to existing benchmark performance data is shown in Exhibit 5.2.

Exhibit 5.2   Sources of Benchmark Performance Data

1. INTERNAL TO THE ORGANIZATION

- Top management
- Stated organizational benchmarks
- Other management and operations personnel
- Customer contacts such as sales personnel, customer service, after service maintenance personnel, and so on
- Surveys and questionnaires
- Purchasing department personnel
- New employees and recently terminated employees
- Planning and budget documents
- Financial and operations reports
- Internal policies, directives, and official memos

2. EXTERNAL FROM THE ORGANIZATION

- Trade journals
- Publications—industry, functional, best practice oriented, and so on
- Professional associations
- Conferences and seminars with materials
- Experts with special industry and functional expertise
- Special newsletters, reports, papers, and so on
- Colleges and universities—faculty, libraries, research, and so on
- Outside consultants—individuals, groups, training materials, and so on
- Competitive analysis—financial and operational
- Clearinghouses—local, national, international
- User groups—computer systems and software, equipment, processes, and so on
- Public domain reports—financial reports, patent records, consumer reports, and so on
- Research papers—industry, practices, innovative approaches, and so on
- Internet—searches, web sites, on-line services, and so on

3. STUDY TEAM RESEARCH

- Direct mail surveys—ex-employees, vendors, customers (present, past and potential)
- Telephone interviews—vendors, customers, employees, and so on
- Consultants—interviews, special training, knowledge sharing, and so on

(continues)

Exhibit 5.2   *(Continued)*

- Observations—company departments, work units, and various locations
- Off-site visits—vendors, customers, competitors, and so on
- Operational reviews—mini-review of organization, department, function, and so on

---

An excellent source of collecting benchmarking data is the Internet. This tool can be used quite easily in the confines of the study team's office. Although there are quite a number of web sites providing data related to benchmarking and benchmarks, some time spent performing a review should disclose those that are most pertinent to the current study. Some of the web sites charge for access to their information, while others require you to be a member of their benchmarking group (at an annual fee that may be thousands of dollars). However, before paying for any of this information, the study team (particularly for smaller organizations) can collect a large amount of benchmark data at no cost.

For instance, a quick search using the search word "benchmarking" resulted in 21,617 matches. The study team would then need to spend the time to further investigate these web sites to determine which ones would be most appropriate for the present study. The internet has made it quite easy to perform initial research and identify best practices prior to initiating the study.

One of the web sites that I am familiar with is The Hackett Group (www.thgi.com) as they work closely with the American Institute of Certified Public Accountants in benchmarking accounting and financial functions of CPA firms and industry. They maintain benchmark databases in the disciplines of finance, human resources, information technology, planning/performance measurement, and procurement. A quick tour of their web site disclosed the following major benchmark findings:

Finance

- Average cost—1.4% of revenue
- Experience—average of 16 years work experience

- Budget completion—average of 95 days with multiple iterations
- Large companies—spend 20 to 40 percent less than smaller companies

Human Resources

- Cost per employee—average of $1,500, more than twice what top performers spend
- Efforts—more than half is devoted to lower value, routine activities
- Employee record changes—average of 2.3 changes per employee annually
- Third party suppliers—average of 16 different third party suppliers

Information Technology

- Range of costs—low end at $3,387 or less per end-user; at high end up to $38,344. The average is $9,218
- Projects on time—more than 40 percent of large projects are delivered late and over budget
- Time spent—half of time spent on operations, end user support, training, and software maintenance. Less than 5 percent is spent planning for the future uses of technology
- Outsourced functions—almost 18 percent of the Information Technology budget. Only 2 percent of time is spent managing outsourcers

Planning/Performance Measurement

- Focus—three-quarters of all performance measures are financially focused
- Budget line items—the average company budgets 230 line items, the best less than 40
- Financial plan development—elapsed time of 4.5 months

- Time to complete a forecast—on average 21 days
- Performance measurements—best companies integrate into planning processes

Procurement

- Costs—the average company spends 1 percent of purchased costs
- Purchases controlled—purchases that represent 40 percent of revenue
- Buying specialists—make up 42 percent of procurement staff
- Time spent—76 percent of time spent on transaction processing
- Suppliers/dollars—90 percent of dollars are directed to only 18 percent of suppliers

While such a quick perusal of benchmarking web sites will not always provide the level of detailed knowledge that the study team is looking for, it can provide numerous starting point data. Should further detailed information be required, the study team could consider a more in-depth analysis of the web site, contacting the benchmarking organization directly for further available information, becoming a member of the benchmarking organization (where the cost would justify the information to be provided), or paying for selected information if possible. Typically, such an internet search is less costly and less time-consuming than other forms of research. Some time should spent on this endeavor in the conducting of an external (and an internal) benchmarking study. With experience, the study team will learn how to make such a search most efficient. Should the study team, or members of the study team, perform additional benchmarking studies, the information obtained through their internet search can be used again. The use of outside consultants may also assist in reducing the amount of the search as the consultants may have already conducted such a search for other clients.

The collection of user-provided original data can be the most important resource to the company's benchmarking study. This typically means the use of a questionnaire and/or personal interviews. For this process to be most successful, study team members must be certain that they are asking the right questions—without any ambiguity. The design of the questionnaire and interview questions is the link between the study team's understanding of the existing critical area for improvement, identified performance gaps, and opportunities for improvement. Each area of questioning must be considered carefully as it is extremely difficult to redo the benchmark study once it is completed. The data collection design should not be undertaken until the benchmark team fully understands the purpose of the benchmark study—what is to be measured and why.

The benchmark team must spend the necessary time to fully understand the critical areas included in the external benchmark study. Members of the study team may have to be trained in such things as benchmarking concepts and principles, the theory of best practices, programs of continuous improvements, operational concepts, good basic business principles, and so on, prior to initiating the study. There should also be sufficient time allotted on the front end of the study to learn about the operational areas included in the study and what might be considered good and bad practices. The study team may also accumulate data relative to known and published best practices so as to provide a framework upon which to analyze those practices found in the companies included in the study. It is incumbent upon the members of the study team to know as much about the companies included in the study and their practices, as well as other existing best practices, prior to the start of the external benchmarking study.

With a knowledgeable study team, the data collected in the actual benchmarking study becomes more valuable. It also makes it much easier for the benchmarking study team to analyze the collected data and arrive at the proper conclusions. The better the study team, the better the external benchmarking study and its results. With the proper study tools and observation techniques, the study can best determine those practices that are unacceptable across companies and those practices that can be considered best practices.

As part of an external competitive benchmarking study, the study team was comparing the number of management personnel that were really required among study participants and how they should spend their time to be most effective. The study team prepared a survey/questionnaire type form for each manager and supervisor to fill out explaining their major departmental and job responsibilities and how each one spent his or her time toward accomplishing expected results. The study team found a consistency across study participants from their own observations and analyzing the results of forms which disclosed the following general patterns and activities:

- Most managers were not quite sure what their specific responsibilities were as managers, so they continued doing the work they had done in their previous positions.
- Those employees classified as supervisors were really chief workers, with minimal authority over the areas they were supposed to supervise.
- There was a general misunderstanding as to why each of their departments existed, and what their role was in helping to accomplish expected results.
- Almost all of the managers and supervisors were not sure what they should be doing with their time, and filled their time by doing the job themselves, policing and controlling those employees reporting to them, or reviewing the work of others and then having the employee redo it their way.
- Over 60 percent of total managers' time (across study participants) was spent on some form of meeting, usually scheduled (an average of over 20 hours per week per manager) by one manager with a large number of other managers in attendance.

The study team sat in on a number of so-called management meetings at each of the study participants' sites and observed that most of the meetings were unnecessary. In fact, the study team found that most of what these managers did was unnecessary or redundant, if the employees were allowed to function on their own. As the study team found no evidence of a best practice with any of the study participants, they decided that they would have to look elsewhere. With proper research, they were able to identify other organizations that did not appear to suffer from the same problems. As a result, the study team was able to develop a best practice recommendation for all of the study participants to consider. It was not a question as to where the best practice came from (it didn't need to be a competitor), but whether it would work in their organization and how to best implement the practice to ensure success.

> *It Is Not the Source of the Best Practice That Is Important, but Whether It Works Best in Your Situation*

The study team should consider all sources for their research. Many times, one source (e.g., an internet web site) may guide the study team to other sources. For instance, a benchmarking web site might reference a specific company or a specific study. The study team might then contact the referenced company or attempt to obtain a copy of the mentioned study. The more knowledge that the study team can accumulate during the data collection phase of the study, the better the results of the study will be. In addition, the more relevant benchmarks that the study team can identify, the greater the chance of developing the ultimate best practices.

QUESTIONNAIRE AND INTERVIEW QUESTIONS DESIGN

The questionnaire for the external benchmarking study should begin with a set of defined objectives. This statement of objectives serves to communicate the purpose, goals, and objectives of the study. Also, the interview questions should first be tested internally as to validity and use looking at such things as:

- Wording and structure of each question as to its purpose
- No ambiguity—each question means the same to all users
- Answerability—can the question really be answered? Easily and simply?
- Willingness to answer—will users answer honestly or at all? Will they be comfortable in answering? Are there any performance drivers that prevent users from answering?
- Self-explanatory—each question is clear with no need for detailed explanations
- Consistency of responses—all responses require no further user interpretation
- Clarity of questioning process and questionnaire document—the document is easy to use and follow, even by someone not part of the area in question
- Use of reinforcement and redundancy between different questions—make sure that all the right questions get answered
- Presentation format—user friendly, allowing for acceptance and ease of use
- Type of question—stick to close-ended questions that can be easily scored, such as yes or no, multiple choice, or specific number/amount
- Objectivity—questions open and clear and not prone to personal opinions and biases
- Availability of data for response—can the responder easily obtain the correct data?
- Separation of process questions from close-end questions. (Many times these questions are separated into two different questionnaires and used at different times.)
- Allowance for further description—for example, process questions
- Ability to record circumstances or justifications for certain answers that may appear to be out of order

A sample external benchmarking questionnaire is shown in Exhibit 5.3.

Exhibit 5.3 Sample External Benchmarking Questionnaire

PURCHASE CYCLE

Purchasing—Receiving—Accounts Payable Functions

I. ORGANIZATIONAL ISSUES

A. How are these functions organized? Hierarchical, vertical, integrated, etc. Provide an organization chart showing positions and personnel.

B. To whom does each function report? Title and name.

C. Who manages each function? Title and name.

D. How many employees in each function?

Purchasing _____, Receiving _____, Accounts Payable _____.

E. What are your major purchasing policies (e.g., dollar limit for central purchasing)? Provide documented policies and procedures.

F. What is the total budget and actual allocation for each function?

G. Do you have functional job descriptions for each position? Provide copies of each one.

II. PURCHASING FUNCTION

A. *Purchase Requisitions* (PRs)

1. How are PRs prepared? Manual form, computer processed, automatic from planning system. Provide a copy of your PR form (blank and filled in).

2. How many PRs were processed in the past fiscal year?

Total Company _____ By Department/Function _____

3. What percent of PRs were returned to users for correction?

4. Do you use computer processing to process PRs to purchase orders (POs)?

5. On average, how quickly can you process a PR to a PO?

6. Do you provide on-line access to open PRs to operating departments and individual requisitioners?

(continues)

191

Exhibit 5.3 *(Continued)*

B. *Purchase Orders* (POs)

1. How are POs prepared? Manual, computer processed, automatic from other systems. Provide a copy of your PO (blank and filled in).

2. How many POs were processed in the past fiscal year?

   Total company _____. By department/function _____.

3. Do you use electronic data transfer (EDT) for any POs?

   What percent of the total? _____

4. On average, how quickly can you process a PO?

5. What is your average number of POs processed?

   By day _____. By employee _____.

6. Do you produce a hard copy PO?

   How many parts? ____ What is the distribution of its parts?

7. Do you provide on-line access to open POs to operating departments and individual requisitioners?

8. What is your cost to process a purchase order?

9. When was the last time this cost was calculated?

10. Is this cost element used in the calculation of inventory reorder quantities?

11. What is your minimal amount for a purchase to be processed through central purchasing? Describe other systems for purchases under this amount.

C. *Vendor Relations, Negotiations, Analysis*

1. What is the total number of vendors in your system?

2. Are your vendors coded by type of commodity class?

3. Can you provide a summary of vendors by commodity class?

   Commodity class _____. Number of vendors _____.

4. How often do you negotiate with vendors? Each purchase, monthly, annually, other.

5. How many vendors make up approximately 80 percent of your total purchases? Can you provide this data of vendors by commodity class?

6. Do you use long-term contracts or blanket purchase orders to lock in price, quality, and on-time deliveries?

Exhibit 5.3 *(Continued)*

---

7. Do you integrate purchases for production raw materials into your production schedule?

8. Do you maintain vendor analysis statistics? Do they include:

   a. Total sales volume

   b. Total sales volume by item

   c. Quality data

   d. Merchandise return data

   e. On-time delivery data

   f. Other

   Provide a sample report(s) of such statistics?

9. Are company individuals assigned contact responsibility for major vendors?

10. How often are long-term purchase contracts renegotiated?

11. Do you have an ongoing process for identification of potential vendors? Describe.

12. How many vendors have you added during the past year?

13. How many vendors have you deleted during the past year?

D. *Open Purchase Order Control and Expediting*

1. How many POs, on average, are open at any one time?

2. Are open POs part of an integrated computer system?

3. Are open POs reported for expediting via this system?

4. Do you use automatic data transmission for open PO expediting? Describe system.

5. Do you expedite on a personal contact basis? Your personnel? Vendor personnel?

6. On average, how many POs are being expedited at one time?

7. On average, how many expedited POs require follow-up calls?

E. *Purchasing Value Analysis*

1. Does the purchasing function have authority to question purchases?

2. Do they have authority to question?

   a. Whether purchase is necessary?

(continues)

Exhibit 5.3 *(Continued)*

---

    b. Quantity to be purchased?

    c. Purchase of less expensive item?

    d. Alternative item to be purchased?

  3. Can they initiate or process changes?

F. *Receiving Function*

  1. On average, what is the total number of open receipts? By PO _____. By item _____.

  2. What types of items or commodity classes does this function receive?

  3. What types of items or commodity classes are received by another manner?

  4. Are open PO receipts part of an integrated computer system?

  5. On average, how many receipts are processed in a day?

  6. Do all such receipts come to a central receiving area? Describe exceptions.

  7. Does the user receive any items directly? What types? Describe procedure.

  8. Are receipts processed by some form of on-line computer system?

  9. Are any receipts processed on a manually prepared form basis? Provide form and describe procedure.

  10. Are receipts part of an integrated computer system?

  11. Do you have a receiving inspection function? Do they inspect all items or by exception? What items are inspected?

  12. On average, how quickly are items routed to users?

  13. Do you use Just in Time (JIT) practices for raw materials?

  14. Are these raw material receipts integrated with your production schedule? Describe process.

  15. Do you have documented receiving procedures? Provide copy of any procedures.

  16. Are open receipts reconciled to open purchase orders? Computer or manual? How often? Percent of errors?

  17. Do you use bar coding in processing your receipts?

  18. What percent of your total receipts are bar coded? Item number? Quantities? Other data?

Exhibit 5.3 *(Continued)*

III. ACCOUNTS PAYABLE

A. *Accounts Payable Processing*

1. On what basis and percents of total payments do you pay vendors?
   a. Pre-pay at time of order
   b. Payment upon receipt
   c. Payment with invoice/receipt within discount terms
   d. Payment with invoice/receipt within 30 days
      • Don't take discount
      • Take discount anyway
   e. Other basis (describe)
2. How often do you process payables for payment?
3. Do you make any exceptions between payment periods?
4. Do you provide for off-line manual vendor payments?
5. On average, what is the amount of new payables at any time? Number of payments? Total dollars?
6. Is accounts payable processing part of an integrated computer system?
7. What is the amount of annual payments? Number of payments? Total dollars?

B. *Open Payables Control*

1. Are open payables part of an integrated computer system?
2. How often do you process payments?
3. Is there a policy to take vendor discounts? Within or at the discount period? Regardless of the discount period?
4. On average, what is the amount of open payables? Number of vendor invoices? Total dollars?
5. Are open payables accessible on an on-line basis? Only accounts payable personnel? Others? (describe)

C. *Vendor Payment Processing*

1. Do you provide a pre-payment listing of due bills prior to processing?
   a. On screen?
   b. Listing only?
   c. Both options?

(continues)

195

Exhibit 5.3 *(Continued)*

---

2. Can an authorized individual select bills for payment?
   a. Manual?
   b. On-line?
   c. Additions?
   d. Deletions?
   e. Changes?
3. Can an authorized individual determine the dollar amount for total payment? What is basis for selection?
4. How often do you process checks for payment? Do you hold to that schedule? How many times did you go off that schedule last year?
5. Do you automatically combine vendor invoices into one payment?
6. Do you provide detail as to what invoices are being paid?
7. Do you reconcile vendor statements to individual invoices?
8. Do you ignore vendor statements and pay only by invoice?
9. Do you automatically net vendor debits against payments?
10. On average, what is the amount of vendor debits?
    Number of debits _____. Total amount _____.
11. Once selected, are checks with payment detail automatically processed? Provide sample of check and detail memo.
12. What is your cost per payment?
13. What is your cost per processing cycle?
14. On average, how many payments do you process at one time? Per process run? Per month? Annually?

D. *Cash Disbursement Processing*
   1. Are payments as processed automatically sent to the vendor? Electronic data transfer? Mail?
   2. How often do you process cash disbursements?
   3. On average, what are the number of checks written?
      By process _____. Monthly _____. Annual _____.
   4. Do you combine payments by vendor? On what basis?
   5. On what basis do you process payment? Receipt of items? Invoice? Both? Other?
   6. Do you use a remote bank location?
   7. Do you use any methods to slow the receipt of the payment to the vendor? Describe.

Exhibit 5.3 *(Continued)*

8. What is your cost per check disbursement? What is your cost per disbursement cycle?

9. How many times have checks been processed late in the last year? Sent out late?

10. What percent of checks have reported errors upon receipt? How many hours and cost are spent in correcting errors?

11. Do you provide electronic data transfer for vendor payments?

12. Is timeliness of payment (e.g., electronic data transfer) considered as a factor in vendor price negotiations?

E. *Record Keeping and Analysis*

1. What records do you keep for each payment?

   a. Purchase requisition

   b. Purchase order

   c. Receiver/bill of lading

   d. Vendor invoice

   e. Payment voucher

   f. Check copy

   g. Other

   h. All computer processed

2. What type of analysis do you do relative to payments?

   a. Payments by vendor: numbers and dollars?

   b. Returns by vendor?

   c. Billing errors?

   d. Processing errors?

   e. Other?

3. Are there other records/analysis that you do? Describe.

4. What report options do you provide?

   a. Standard in software?

   b. Custom defined?

   c. User?

5. What software do you use for these functions?

6. What computer hardware configuration do you use? Provide details.

> ## *Hope Springs Eternal*
> ## *as We Identify More Benchmarks*

MEASUREMENT SYSTEMS AND TECHNIQUES

Although there may be a tendency to rely on intuition and gut feelings in analyzing benchmarking data, data integrity and accuracy are extremely important in maintaining the credibility of the study and ensuring proper results. Benchmarking data may tend to be soft, leading to quick conclusions, especially where the company and/or the study team want to save time and money. Therefore, it is extremely important that the study team use the best data sources possible as they conduct the benchmarking study. There are a number of methods to capture benchmarking data, each one presenting its own strengths, weaknesses, and level of precision.

Direct Data Measurement

This method relates to data collection systems where events, activities, and transactions can be recorded via computer processing. Such data collection is typically very accurate as it records data as it is actually happening. Usually, this data is the best measure due to its accuracy, comparability, and reliability of results. Examples of this type of data include number of checks written, number of bills processed, receipts, shipments, work-in-process (WIP) moves, and so on.

Indirect Data Measurement

This method relates to data collection when the data is not collected at the actual time that the event, activity, or transaction occurs. For example, when certain receiving data is not collected at the time of the receipt such as receiver, time of processing, errors in receipt, vendor location, etc. As an alternative, you may have to go back to the original receiving documents where this information is recorded. This method is usually not as reliable as the direct method since it depends on the accuracy of the original documents and some of these documents may be missing elements of data or missing entirely.

Statistical Samples

This method can develop estimates when complete and accurate data may be missing. For instance, there may be a large number of transactions without sufficient data collected to reach a conclusion. Statistical sampling can determine an approximate hit or error rate; for example, the average number of sales contacts per customer that results in a sales order.

Interviewing and Observation

Interviewing and observation techniques can be helpful to reinforce or clarify data collected by other means, or where other methods are not practical. While these methods can be quite helpful, particularly in the understanding of processes, functions, and activities; they can result in subjective data. Therefore, they should not be used exclusively, but together with the recording of actual transactions.

> ## Doing the Right Things, the Right Ways

Exhibit 5.4 displays a list of some sample benchmarking measures.

Exhibit 5.4   Sample Benchmarking Measures

SALES FORECASTS

1. Forecast to Actual: Total, by Customer, by Salesperson, by Product
2. Forecast to Real Customer Orders
3. Forecast: This Year to Last Year

(continues)

Exhibit 5.4 *(Continued)*

4. Forecast to Lost Orders

5. Customer Contacts: Number, Type, Results

6. Reliability: Amount of Real Customer Orders, Right Product to Right Customer at Right Time

7. Integration: With Company Plans, Manufacturing, Engineering, Accounting

8. Flexible: To Customer, Company Capacity, Sales and Revenue Plans

SALES ORDER BACKLOG

1. Sales Order to Production Order: Time Processed

2. Average Time in Backlog

3. Reduction in Backlog: Current, Compared to Past

4. Backlog Statistics: Conversion to Real Orders, Number and Amount of Lost Orders

5. Timeliness: Length of Time in Backlog, Inability to get into Production

6. Type of Backlog: By Product, by Salesperson, by Complexity, by Process Required

7. Coordination: Sales, Manufacturing, Engineering

8. Control: With Production Schedule, Other Commitments, Outside Sources

MANUFACTURING ORDERS

1. Average Processing Time: Sales Order Receipt to Manufacturing Order

2. Timeliness into Production: Per Schedule, Production Ready

3. Timeliness of Start: Materials on Time, Production Start

4. Movement Through Work in Process: Timeliness, Queue Time, Move Time

5. Comparison to Standards: Material, Labor, Scrap, Rejects, Rework

6. Quality Control: Number of Inspections, Rejects

7. Receiving: Personnel, Time, Process

8. Shipping: Process, Timeliness, Method, Costs

Exhibit 5.4   *(Continued)*

9. Delivery: On Time, Customer Satisfaction, Returned Items
10. Process: Smooth Flow, Minimal Paperwork, Fully Automated

INVENTORY

1. Raw Material: Amount Just in Time, Amount on Hand, Amount Decreased
2. Work in Process: Maximize Throughput, Schedule Versus Actual, Percentage Just in Time, Number Completed on Time
3. Finished Goods: Completed on Time, Shipped Directly, Amount
4. Records: Physical to Records, Type of Data/Reporting
5. Statistics: Turnover, Obsolete, Inaccuracies
6. Items in Inventory: Number at Zero Inventory, Amount of Excess Inventory
7. Process: Zero Inventory, Material Requirements Planning, Statistical Analysis (Reorder Points And Reorder Quantities)
8. Organization: Smooth Flow, Minimal Receipts and Issues, Minimal Paperwork

PURCHASING

1. Process Type: Direct, Purchase Orders, Electronic Data Transfer, Blanket Purchases
2. Numbers: Purchase Orders, Personnel, Vendors
3. Timeliness: Purchase Requisitions to Purchase Orders, Purchase Orders to Vendor
4. Vendor Relations: Number, Personnel, Negotiations
5. Vendor Statistics: Prices, Quality, Timeliness, Purchase Data
6. Expediting: Open Purchases, Time and Cost, Late Deliveries

ENGINEERING

1. Bill of Materials: Accuracy, Number of Changes
2. Specifications: Accuracy, Number of Specifications
3. Timeliness: New Products, Change Orders
4. Costs: New Design, Change Orders, Maintenance

(continues)

Exhibit 5.4   *(Continued)*

BILLING, ACCOUNTS RECEIVABLE, AND COLLECTIONS

1. Billings: Timeliness, Accuracy, Process, Cost
2. Method of Preparation: Manual, Computer Processing, Electronic Data Transfer
3. Billing Cycle Time: Preparation, Mail, Receipt by Customer
4. Personnel: Number, Time per Bill, Staff Versus Managers
5. Collections: Days Outstanding, Cost per Dollar Collected
6. Bad Debts: To Sales, Amount
7. Cash Receipts: Process, Time to Deposit, Average Days
8. Credit: Process, Approvals, Over and Under Limits
9. Invoices Returned: Bad Addresses, Inaccuracies

ACCOUNTS PAYABLE

1. Process: Direct Pay, Electronic Data Transfer, Computer Processing, Manual
2. Payments: Number, Timeliness, Accuracy, and Errors
3. Costs: Per Payment, Personnel, Distribution, Mailing
4. Payment Errors: Number, Costs
5. Discounts: Taken, Lost, Costs
6. Efficiency: Smooth Processing, Fully Automated, Minimal Manual Processing

PAYROLL

1. Process: Method, Internal or External, Frequency, Distribution
2. Process Errors: Number, Type, Costs, Correction Methods
3. Employee Benefits: Number, Type, Costs
4. Reporting: Frequency, Media, Accuracy, Timeliness
5. Costs: Per Employee, per Check
6. Record Keeping: Fully Automated, No Duplications, Adequate Information

ACCOUNTING AND FINANCIAL

1. Reporting: Late Reports, Errors in Reports, Not Needed
2. Outside Auditors: Cost, Timeliness, Errors Found, Benefits

Exhibit 5.4   *(Continued)*

3. Errors: Process, Personnel, Costs to Correct

4. Data Entry Errors: Number and Percent by Application

5. Journal Entries: Automatic Computer Processed, Manual, Number, Correcting Entries

6. Cost: Per General Ledger Journal Entry Transaction

7. Budgets: To Plan, to Actual, to What It Should Be

8. Process: Fully Automated, Minimal Manual Interventions, Adequate Information

PERSONNEL

1. Organization: Number of Personnel, Functions

2. Costs: Departmental, per Employee, per Function

3. Processing: In-house or Outside, Level of Inclusion

4. Result Statistics: Hires, Training, Orientation, Discharges

5. Employee Benefits: Type, Number, Administration

6. Benefits Versus Costs: Hiring, Orientation, Training, Evaluations, Discharges

INTERPRETING BENCHMARKING STUDY RESULTS

After tabulating and analyzing the benchmarking data collected, the study team can document those functional areas and practices where the company is:

- An above-average performer—little or no improvement needed.
- About equal with benchmarked companies—improvement desired for competitive advantage?
- Substandard in performance—what level of improvement do the stakeholders desire?
- Data indecisive or not comparable to the company—may desire to conduct further study or additional research.

In developing the company's program for continuous improvements, the study team must look at various factors that may impact upon the level of improvements, if any, that may be desired, such as:

- Substandard performance may actually be desired and negative results may actually be positive. For example, a company with a high regard for customer service that benchmarks as paying too much for customer service activities may see such results as reassuring that they are doing something right. They may, however, want to look at these costs.
- What is the company's intent versus the other benchmarking participants? Right and wrong practices may be relative to the situation.
- Whether the company is:
  ❏ Doing the right things the wrong way.
  ❏ Doing the wrong things the wrong way.
  ❏ Doing the wrong things the right way.
  ❏ Doing the right things the right way.
- The diverse needs of stakeholders such as:
  ❏ Vendors wanting payment on time.
  ❏ Employees wanting to be treated fairly.
  ❏ Customers wanting quality products, on time, at least cost.
  ❏ Owners/stockholders wanting to maximize their return.
- Accurate identification of performance gaps and relative prioritization of each one. What is the significance and criticalness of each performance gap. Which ones are important enough to warrant immediate attention, which ones can be taken care of later, and which ones are not relative? For example, a product enhancement gap resulting in large loss of market share could be survival threatening and must be addressed immediately; while a reduction in after the sale customer service to cut costs may never be desirable.

Enright Electronics had prospered due to its development of a proprietary product used in personal computer motherboards. Last year their patent had run out and competitors were selling much less expensive copies. This resulted in running Enright's profits into the ground. Enright had relied on this one product as the base of its business and had not been able to develop another such profitable product during the course of the patent period. Enright management had done everything that they could think of internally (including an internal benchmarking study) to save the company. They came up with some short-term stop gap measures, but profits kept fading. They decided to host an external benchmarking study with three of their competitors—hoping to learn from their competitors how to operate more economically, efficiently, and effectively.

When the Enright company management looked at the results of the external benchmarking study, they were appalled. Their employee morale was the lowest as were their sales and percentage of the market. They had been the leader in market share just three years ago. Their competitors had all become off-shore purchasers and resellers. This was how they kept their costs and selling prices down while increasing profits. This was the best practice for the industry. Enright management rejected this practice on ethical terms. They believed that they owed something to their employees and vendors. They refused to downsize and move their manufacturing offshore on a low-cost contract basis. As things stood, there wasn't much else that could be done to save the company.

> ## A Fool and His Obstinancy
> ## Are Soon Bankrupt

The one thing that Enright still possessed was their name in the marketplace, which had always stood for quality products and service. Enright management had the option of selling the company while they could still get a decent price for it. The external benchmarking study had revealed that two of their competitors had grown through acquisitions and might be interested in buying Enright. Enright management rejected this option as well as the other findings of the external benchmarking study and six months later they were in bankruptcy. They still had their ethics and honor, but the creditors had the company.

ANALYZING BENCHMARKING RESULTS

The external benchmarking team gathers information from various areas such as data source review, questionnaire responses from benchmarking participants, interviews and operational reviews of other operations, discussions with internal and external experts, and so on. From the data collected, the benchmarking team integrates the data obtained with the knowledge/information gained from its internal benchmarking operational review. The goal of this effort is to identify those areas where the company is performing well and possible improvement may be desired, and those areas where immediate improvements can be implemented or where future effort may be placed.

Six steps which should be used to analyze benchmarking results:

1. Compare company performance drivers and benchmarking data—documenting similarities and differences between the company and study participants such as economics, geography, special events/transactions (e.g., write-offs, disasters), size of company/division/location, regulations and laws, local customs, policies and procedures, benefits, practices, and so on.

2. Categorize, classify, and analyze the quantitative data. Prepare easily understood comparison charts. The data itself, charts and graphs, and narratives can be used for this purpose. The study team should document the relevance of each factor to the company and its operations.

3. Review and analyze qualitative data such as questionnaire and interview/operational review comments to identify any additional performance gaps, best practices, innovative practices, unique approaches, and areas for further study.

4. Recontact or revisit individuals or companies, where necessary, to confirm and finalize the study team's findings and conclusions.

5. Compare the results of the qualitative review to quantitative data and make any necessary adjustments to findings. Document the analysis and its impact on study results.

6. Communicate the findings and results of the external benchmarking study to the benchmarking team, internal personnel, and benchmarking participants. The study team does not need to provide their data analysis to benchmarking participants unless previously agreed in the participant agreement. Otherwise, data tabulations (including your company's data) without naming participants should be sufficient.

Organizations should be established so that each individual, from the lowest to the highest level, can flourish professionally and personally and move toward their real potential within the organization. This is what could be called a healthy organization, characterized by a working-together rather than a working-for atmosphere and a cooperative rather than a competitive environment. The establishment of the organization reflects management's mental models and belief systems and establishes the performance drivers by which employees work and achieve results. In a healthy organization, all individuals should know clearly what is expected of them and account for achieving the agreed results—working in a self-motivated disciplined behavior modality. This philosophy would constitute a set of organizational benchmarks on which to compare the company against others in an external benchmarking study—looking for best practices in a program of continuous improvements.

Apex Industries was a typical hierarchical organization where the reward carrot was movement up the management ranks. There was intense interdepartmental competition and each department saw the budget as their own domain. In effect, each department was trying to get as much of the total budget pie for themselves as they could, regardless of their own needs. Individuals and departments within the organization progressed by putting down the others, rather than impressing through their own accomplishments. Everybody had a bad word about everyone else and bad feelings prevailed throughout the organization. Apex had become one of the most oppressive back-biting organizations in the industry. Top management had embraced the organizational benchmarks as stated above, but they had never become reality. Now that business had dropped substantially with sales down and costs up, they were desirous of making changes. They decided that an external benchmarking study with their three major competitors might provide some guidance for them as to others' best practices.

The results of the external benchmarking study disclosed that Apex's operating practices and processes were comparable to their competitors. While there were some improvements that could be made by implementing best practices, it really wasn't their systems that was the problem, it was their people. When the other organizations in the external benchmarking study were compared, the company with the best results in sales, costs, and profits was the closest to meeting what Apex management believed was their organizational benchmarks as to how the organization should function. The other company had created a working-together atmosphere in which each employee cooperated to achieve individual and group results.

We Need to Rethink, Before We Can Relearn

Apex management understood the other company's organizational processes and practices—it was exactly what they said they desired—but they had no idea how to implement such procedures. Management suggested a number of methods for implementation from selling the business and starting over with new employees, getting rid of most of the present employees and outsourcing, gross layoffs and re-hiring, firing the personnel department, and so on.

Suddenly, one of the middle managers got up and wrote on the flipchart in big letters R-E-S-P-E-C-T. The other managers nodded their heads affirmatively. The difficult part was making it work.

IDENTIFYING BEST PRACTICES

Now that the study team has gathered, analyzed, and prioritized the data collected; they are now ready to present their findings as to which organization (including their own company) has the best practice in which area. There may be more than one organization with best practices, and one organization may be best in a number of categories. Often, the organization with the best practice is not compatible to the study team's company and they need to look at the second- or third-best practice to find the right practice to fit their situation. Typically, the external benchmarking team will use charts, graphs, and other visuals to present their findings as to best practices and related performance gaps compared to their company.

The study team has various sources of substantiation to back up their conclusions as to which study has the best practice, the next best, and so on. It is not merely a summarization of numeric data but also a decision based on such things as observation, operational review techniques, personal interviews (management and operations personnel), survey forms, questionnaires, data analysis, and so on. Based on these data sources, the study team summarizes their findings and conclusions. While such findings may be presented in summary form, the external benchmarking team must be sufficiently knowledgeable to present and explain each company's practices in detail—depicting their advantages and disadvantages, strengths and weaknesses, relationship to the study company, and so on. Often, the overall best practice is a composite of what the study company is presently doing together with the pieces of best practice from the other study participants.

The study team should not blindly recommend a best practice strictly based on the reporting of numerical data or subjective preference. Any best practice recommended should incorporate the best systems and procedures that can be replicated from the composite of company practices included in the study. The knowledge of benchmarking study team members, other sources, research, and good business sense can also enhance developed best practices. Once a best practice is selected and implemented, the practice is continually subject to review and improvement. Remember the goal of external benchmarking is not merely to match the best practice of your competitors but to surpass them.

Some examples of best practice presentations are shown in Exhibit 5.5.

Exhibit 5.5 Examples of Best Practice Presentations

1. *Time to Process a Sales Order to a Manufacturing Order*

Company	Time	Rank
Our Company	4 days	3rd
ABC Company	6 days	4th
DEF Company	3 days	2nd
HGI Company	1 day	1st (Best)

2. Cost of Sales to Sales Department Cost

Company	Cost	Rank
Our Company	$ .45	1st (Best)
ABC Company	.57	3rd
DEF Company	.52	2nd
HGI Company	.78	4th

3. Cost to Process a Sales Order

Company	Cost	Rank
Our Company	$8.84	2nd
ABC Company	6.56	1st (Best)
DEF Company	10.37	4th
HGI Company	9.74	3rd

Exhibit 5.5 *(Continued)*

4. Percentage of Errors in Sales Orders

Company	% Errors	Rank
Our Company	6.8%	4th
ABC Company	2.8%	2nd
DEF Company	2.2%	1st (Best)
HGI Company	3.6%	3rd

Organizations tend to operate based on company policies, which are rightfully set by those in top management to establish the tone or atmosphere for the organization to do its business. These policies help to establish the mental models, belief systems, and performance drivers on which the company operates. For instance, policies may be established that set up a loose framework of operations, such as site- or department-based management where each company segment operates in its own way. On the other hand, policies may dictate a tight centrally-controlled management structure where headquarters management must approve all expenditures over a certain amount (e.g., $1,000). Top management may see the right to establish policies over those they employ as its responsibility. Sometimes these policies are formally written in impressive-looking tomes and other times they are informal whims of top management as the employees interpret.

Scope Industries was one of those organizations who operated all facets of their business under the cloak of distinct policies. The company had an eight-person department whose sole job was to document (and repeatedly change) and distribute company policies. This group was the communication link between top management and the rest of the company. Top management wanted a formal documented policy on every aspect of the company's operations. Management and operations personnel were then held accountable for all such policies.

One of the company's divisions, located at a site some distance from company headquarters, had all sorts of problems trying to operate according to strict company policies. The division manager, who was held accountable for division operating results, was adamant that the division could not operate effectively under such company policies. This division was located in a small rural town of less than 100,000 population, where most of the employees had previously been farmers and many still were. Company headquarters was located in a large urban east coast city of over two million people, where there was a sufficient labor pool. The urban employees were willing to follow strict company policies as a requirement of their jobs.

Many of the strict company policies got in the way of day-to-day operations at the remote operating divisions. For instance, there was a company policy to support the local economy by purchasing through local suppliers whenever possible. However, all purchase orders and subsequent payments had to be processed and approved by company headquarters purchasing personnel. This delay made it difficult to work with local vendors and many of these vendors who were used to a more cash-and-carry type arrangement, chose not to deal with the company. The company policy as to official starting and quitting times caused an unnecessary burden on employees at the division level. Many of these employees had to tend their farms the first thing in the morning, while other employees had personal or family commitments prior to quitting time or had a large number of miles to travel. This policy had caused the division to lose a number of good employees as well as rendering it unable to hire certain individuals.

There was also an unwritten policy management employees must dress in an appropriate business suit with a tie and jacket when working for the company on or off site. This policy not only caused employee and management separation, but also caused great dissension as many employees were related or lived in the same rural area.

It was apparent that such strict company policies had an adverse affect on this division's operations. Top management believed that they were correct in instituting such strict company policies within the organization. They could not see any other method of control over such remote operations. However, as top management continued to see an ongoing deterioration of results at each of their locations, they were willing to participate in an external benchmarking study with four of their competitors to determine if there were better practices.

The results of the external benchmarking study disclosed that none of their competitors had strict company policies in place and none of them had a policy writing group. The company with the best results as to sales, costs, and profits operated under a concept of broad guidelines and directions from top management. They left the implementation of finite operating systems and procedures to those responsible for the operating division. There was no competition between operating divisions and locations, only competition within each division to be the best they could. In effect, each division competed only against itself. Top management at Scope agreed with the study results and the possibility of changing certain policies that just were not practical or did not make sense at the division level. However, they were not ready to disband the company Policies and Procedures Group (PPG). When the operating division moved to change certain policies consistent with the results of the external benchmarking study, top management told them that they would have to clear such changes with PPG. When the division managers presented their changes to PPG, they were told that they would have to get prior approval from top management. While top management agreed to the results of the external benchmarking study, they were not willing to do what had to be done to implement best practices. They could not give up the old company's never-ending cycle of back and forth with no results.

> ## *Do the Right Thing—*
> ## *Forget the Policies and Procedures*

The external benchmarking study exercise is not merely a process of documenting the host company's and other study participants' best practices, but also requires the identification of the manner in which they can best be implemented within the company. Such implementation procedures must be part of the study team's presentation, clearly describing what needs to change to make the best practice work. As the above example shows, such implementation may be different for each segment of the organization. In addition, what works best for one organization may have to be altered to work best for your organization, considering such things as mental models, belief systems, performance drivers, management and employee attitudes, and so on.

SITE VISIT OBSERVATIONS AND PROCESS ANALYSIS

Once the external benchmarking team, company management, and operations personnel have agreed as to the company(ies) with the best practices, the study team will probably want to visit these sites to analyze their processes to see if they can use these best practices to improve their own operations. Examples of four practice criteria and the corresponding need for off-site observation follow:

1. Time to Process a Sales Order to a Manufacturing Order. Company HGI processes their sales orders in only one day, possibly because of practices which the study company can not do. Therefore, the study team may also need to visit DEF which takes three days to process a sales order, but which is more comparable to the study company.
2. Cost of Sales to Sales Department Cost. While the study company appears to be the best in this practice, the study team believes that there are certain things that the company is not doing which could increase its desired sales without appreciable additional costs. Therefore, the study team should visit ABC and DEF to analyze their processes.
3. Cost to Process a Sales Order. The study company comes up second in this practice. The study team should visit ABC which shows the best cost, and possibly also visit DEF to determine methods and practices to reduce the study company's costs even further.

4. Percentage of Errors in Sales Orders. The study company is the worst in this practice area, and it could learn something from each of the others. It would probably be to the company's benefit for the study team to visit all of the other companies.

The external benchmarking team can use survey forms, questionnaires, interviews, flowcharts, layout diagrams, and so on to collect their data during such site visits. If the study team visits more than one company to address the same practice, they need to make sure that the team's data collection tools are consistent. Typically, the benchmarking team will document their findings in a formal written report, as well as presenting their findings orally to management and operations personnel. When reporting, the study team can include information on the following:

- Additional data, statistics, and circumstances which may not have been included in the initial data gathering
- Organization structure and personnel considerations
- Facilities, equipment, and layout considerations
- Data collection and information systems
- Source documents, forms, and reports used
- Special processes used such as direct payment systems, electronic data transfer, bar code reading, computer processing, and so on
- Policies and procedures which enhance the practice
- Business climate enhancements and unique practices
- Mental models, belief systems, and performance drivers which enhance a best practice at another company
- Special positive factors or considerations relative to another company's operations

PROCESS COMPARISONS

Many times in an external benchmarking study, the study team finds that other companies perform the same practice as the host company, using a different process. It is always good for the study team to understand how different organizations solve the same problem as their company more effectively and how their company can better use such practices. In addition, it allows the study team to relate another company's practice (the best and others) with their own present processes. This technique known as process comparison can also provide a quick picture of how study participants approach similar situations and how the host company can fill a performance gap. The study team would need to consider those factors which allow the other company to be more effective. This could be a difference in belief systems, personnel, work practices, organizational structure, management styles, and so on.

The study team needs to be aware that just because another company uses a different practice or process more effectively than the host company, it doesn't mean that the host company can adapt such practices easily. The host company may need to make organizational and other changes before it can implement the same practices effectively. Examples of such process comparisons are shown in Exhibit 5.6.

Exhibit 5.6   Process Comparison Examples

Type Of Process	Study Participant			
	Us	ABC	DEF	GHI
1. *Time: Sales Order to Manufacturing Order*				
• Electronic ordering	NO	NO	Y/N	YES
• Repetitive ordering	Y/N	NO	Y/N	YES
• Integration	NO	NO	YES	YES
2. *Cost of Sales to Sales Department Cost*				
• Inside and outside sales	NO	YES	YES	YES
• Direct write-up	YES	NO	NO	NO
• Customer sales orders	YES	NO	YES	NO

Exhibit 5.6 *(Continued)*

Type Of Process	*Study Participant*			
	Us	*ABC*	*DEF*	*GHI*
3. *Cost to Process a Sales Order*				
• Sales desk	YES	YES	NO	NO
• Electronic ordering	NO	NO	Y/N	YES
• Order form scanning	YES	YES	NO	YES
4. *Percentage of Errors in Sales Orders*				
• Computer checking	NO	YES	YES	NO
• Customer echo check	NO	NO	YES	NO
• Standard product codes	NO	YES	NO	NO

With reference to process comparisons, one of the questions that always seems to arise as part of the external benchmarking study is how many managers and supervisors there should be in the organization. The tendency always seems to make more and more managers. There seems to be an unwritten rule in many organizations that after so many years with the organization, each employee earns the right to become a manager. If the employee is not promoted to manager, there must be something wrong with him or her. This internal pressure to have everyone eventually rise to at least the level of manager has resulted in costly and inefficient over-managing and some undisciplined behavior at the employee level. The answer to the question of how many managers there should be in any given organization is none—if the company can get away with it. It's not managers, *per se*, who are needed, but the exercise of the management functions, and self-motivated disciplined employees can do these much more effectively.

The Acme Company was a large regional manufacturer of consumer products. As part of an external benchmarking study with three of their competitors, it was concerned about respective organizational structures and how it could operate with less personnel at less cost, be more efficient, and produce increased results. Of over

120 employees, Acme had 24 managers and supervisors plus eight Vice Presidents, four Division Directors, and the President—37 management employees out of 120 or over 30 percent. It was obvious that Acme was over-managed and supervised. Acme management didn't want to apply a quick fix such as arbitrary downsizing or indiscriminate layoffs. They wanted to see if any of their competitors had a more effective process.

> ## *It's Not an Exercise of How Many Managers Can Fit on an Organization Chart, but How Few Are Really Needed*

Acme management had always embraced a mental model that they called "the theory of seven." This theory related to an individual's capacity for span of control. They believed that no work unit of seven employees or more can function properly without supervision or management, and conversely no manager can effectively control more than seven employees. For years, this system worked if control was the only criteria. These were also years when the company made more than adequate profits in spite of itself. Now that aggressive competitors had entered the marketplace and the market share had eroded, Acme was concerned that maybe there was a better process for managing. As a result of the external benchmarking study, Acme management realized that they were the most inefficient when it came to the numbers of managers and productivity per employee. Through site visits, observations, and assistance from the study participants, they learned how to combine work groups and eliminate most of the managers and supervisors. They became more efficient at less cost. By motivating individual employee-disciplined behavior, they were able to eliminate 20 of the 24 manager and supervisor positions. Some of these managers and supervisors went back to work, some became coaches and facilitators, and some were helped out of the company. Acme management now embraced "the theory of one," each employee is responsible for his or her own set of expectations and results.

BENCHMARKING BEYOND THE STUDY

It is quite possible that the benchmarking team may not find a legitimate best practice as a result of their external benchmarking study. If it is a competitive study, the study team may find that all of the study participants, including the host company, are operating under less than desirable practices. Rather than implement a best practice merely because it is the best in the study (less inefficient than the others), the study team needs to investigate further. They could increase the competitive study to include additional participants, increase the scope of the study toward a more encompassing industry study, or add the elements of a best-in-class study for this particular function or activity.

It is always important for the members of the study team to know as many best practices as possible as they conduct their benchmarking study. They should also be aware of the specific goals of top management (and other managers and operating personnel) for the functions included in the benchmarking study. Sometimes members of the study team come with such previous knowledge, other times they acquire it during the research or data collection phases of the study, and still other times they need to be trained or indoctrinated as to the universe of best practices.

To assist the study team in this endeavor of identifying best practices, the following partial lists of best practices are presented by function or activity:

Organization

- The least number of people as possible
- The least amount of management as possible
- The use of self-motivated disciplined behavior by employees
- The concept of coaches and facilitators, rather than watchers
- Each function or activity organized in the optimum manner
- Organization based on the three Es—economy, efficiency, and effectiveness
- Integration of functions to foster cooperation rather than competition

219

- Authority delegated to the lowest possible level
- Compensation based on results, not by seniority or subjectively
- Elimination of all non-value-added functions or activities

Sales

- Realistic sales forecasts related to real customer orders
- Selling the right product, to the right customer, at the right time
- Sales forecasts directly related to the organization's business plan
- Integration with other functions such as manufacturing, engineering, and accounting
- Compensation system produces desired goals of the sales function
- Customer service, rather than a sales, orientation
- Selling to good customers—present and potential
- Provide a feedback mechanism back to the company from customers

Planning and Budgeting

- Planning system to include strategic plans, long-term plans, short-term plans (organizational and departmental), and detail plans
- Planning system to embrace a top-to-bottom, and bottom-to-top process
- Planning process to be continual, not a one-time, static activity (e.g., annually)
- Plans to include the definitions of organizational benchmarks
- Top management to provide direction for the company, others to move in those directions with the ability to measure results
- Budgets to be integrated with the planning system so that they become the dollar allocations of the plan

- Budgets to be flexible so they automatically change as the plan changes
- Budgets to help the company reach their profit plan, not set up as a constrainer or an organizational straight jacket
- Budgets to be reported as progress against an agreed plan
- Actual expenditures compared to what they should be, not merely to the budget

Manufacturing

- Committed to the processing of real customer orders, not for inventory
- Production schedule a reality
- Customer orders entered into production on time
- Minimize inventories (pushing toward zero inventory) for raw materials, work in process, and finished goods
- Customer orders completed and shipped on time
- Productivity maximized at the least cost: set ups, processing, moves, and so on
- Plant capacity optimized with over and under capacity conditions considered effectively
- Peripheral activities minimized such as quality control, receiving, shipping, storeroom operations, maintenance
- Production worker responsibility: quality control, maintenance, moves, and so on
- Elimination of rework, rejects, and scrap

Purchasing

- Least amount possible
- Elimination of all unnecessary paperwork such as purchase requisitions and purchase orders
- Effective vendor negotiations as to price, quality, and timeliness
- Large repetitive orders established through electronic ordering

- Small purchases excluded from the central purchasing system by such methods as petty cash, cash ordering, credit cards, and vendor agreements
- Maximum use of electronic data transfers
- Value analysis procedures that question all major purchases
- Self-purchasing by departments based on agreed plans

Accounting and Finance

- Elimination of all unnecessary functions or activities
- Less mechanical record-keeping and more analysis
- Integration of operating data with financial data
- Use of effective cost accounting system which results in effective cost reductions and identification of trouble spots—by product, by function, and by customer
- Payment of vendor invoices at the time of material receipt to eliminate accounts payable and related costs
- Receipt of customer payment at the time of shipping or delivery to eliminate accounts receivable and related costs
- Payroll processing and record-keeping accomplished at the lowest possible cost—either in-house or outsourced
- Timely provision of financial and operating information with proper analysis
- Use of computer processing and electronic data transfers to the extent possible
- Concept of accounting and financial functions as a business adviser (and profit center) rather than a reporter of financial data and a cost center

Other Areas

- Credit policies that allow the organization to sell only to good customers
- Effective hiring, orientation, training, evaluation, promotion, and firing procedures
- Minimization of non-value-added activities

- Ongoing program of continuous improvements and best practices
- All operations conducted under the principles of the three Es
- Minimization of management, support, and administrative functions
- Rewards based on achieved results
- Effective reporting systems that assist in identifying trouble spots and their causes
- Cooperative working rather than a competitive working atmosphere
- Continual development of a learning organization

The above items are only meant as starting points. The list should be filled in based on the organization's requirements. Specific best practices could also be categorized and accumulated. In addition, existing practices should be continually reviewed and analyzed to ensure that they are achieving their intended purposes. For instance, a customer service response system was established for immediate customer contact and assistance. Initially, there were individuals waiting at telephones for customer calls. This system was replaced with a voice mail system which allows the customer to hold on the line or leave a message. While this system is less costly, it may not achieve the original goal of customer services. The real goal, of course, is to eliminate all customer calls by providing the quality in the first place.

> ## Best Practices Are Those That Achieve the Desired Results

In addition to acquainting themselves with the above best practice guidelines by function, the external benchmarking team of the host company should also accumulate those best practices that they become aware of, regardless of the source. Some of these best practices may be implemented solely through a minor systems or policy change. For example, instituting a performance bonus for all employees who meet or exceed their expected results on a periodic basis. Other best practices may require more extensive changes prior to implementation such as a change in a belief system (e.g., casual Fridays). Still others may not be appropriate for the organization at the present moment (e.g., eliminating the accounts payable function) but should be filed away for future referral and applicability.

To create a proper framework on which to evaluate the appropriateness of a best practice, the study team should know the basic businesses the company is in and the best practice goals for those endeavors. For instance, the basic guidelines and best practice goals for the cash conversion and customer service businesses.

Cash Conversion Business

The stated goal of the cash conversion business is to minimize the infusion of cash and maximize the return of cash so that the return of cash exceeds the infusion of cash by the largest amount possible (e.g., net profits). To effectively accomplish this in a positive manner, the company must:

- Minimize investment in assets (e.g., accounts receivable, inventory, plant and equipment)
- Maximize retention of liabilities without sacrificing operating results (e.g., accounts payable, taxes payable, and so on)
- Maximize increase in stockholder's equity (e.g., net profits and retained earnings)

To accomplish the above goals successfully, there are numerous practices that the company could consider for implementation including the following:

- Minimize or eliminate the level of accounts receivable through the following practices:
  - ❏ Collect amounts due from customers at the time of shipment or delivery (or in advance if possible).

❏ Reduce the time necessary for collections. Each day's reductions is that amount in the company's pocket.

❏ Sell only to good customers, those that pay timely within the period due.

❏ Use electronic data transfer to eliminate customer mailings, company mail receipts, accounts receivable processing, and collection activities.

❏ Eliminate the accounts receivable function through direct payment upon shipping or receipt by the major customers. Calculate the cost of the accounts receivable and collections functions and pass the cost savings on to the customer in terms of reduced prices. There is a price at which the customer will be willing to pay prior to or upon receipt of the goods or services.

❏ Calculate the total cost of billing, accounts receivable processing, and collection activities. For all sales under that total amount, collect in advance or at time of delivery. Pass the processing cost savings onto the customer in part or in full.

• Minimize the cost and levels of inventory through the following practices:

❏ Raw material inventories:

- Negotiate with vendors as to delivering raw materials "just in time," as needed for entry into production.

- Integrate the purchasing function into the production schedule so that vendor commitments and delivery schedules are coordinated with the start of production.

- Receive raw materials directly into production, bypassing the receiving function, incoming inspection, and raw material storerooms.

- Assign responsibility for receiving raw materials directly into production to production personnel.

- Automatically release raw material purchase commitments from vendors via some form of electronic messaging based on the production schedule.

❏ Work in process inventories:
  - Initiate real customer orders into production based on customer required delivery dates.
  - Do not start a manufacturing order into production before it is necessary.
  - Minimize the amount of time any order remains in production to the least amount of time as possible.
  - Maximize the number of good completed items in production.
  - Minimize or eliminate the amount of scrap, rework, or rejects.
  - Reduce the number of moves and the amount of time an order waits in the queue between manufacturing operations.
  - Reduce or eliminate the number and amount of production set-ups.
  - Improve overall productivity by increasing processing times.

❏ Finished goods inventories:
  - Maximize the number of completed manufacturing orders as to being real customer orders rather than finished goods inventory.
  - Ship directly from production, bypassing finished goods inventory entirely.
  - Automatically bill the customer at the time of completion.
  - Minimize the amount of returned items through production quality.

• Minimize the amount of investment in property, plant, and equipment through the following practices:
  ❏ Invest in the minimal level of property, plant, and equipment that is normally needed, not too little and not too much.
  ❏ Develop safety nets for times of over and under plant capacity.
    - Over capacity (that is too much plant)—subcontract for

others, perform preventive maintenance, rent out excess space, and so on.

- Under capacity (that is not enough plant)—subcontract to others, adjust work schedules, bring in part-time personnel, add an extra partial or full shift, and so on.
- Use space in a judicious and orderly fashion so that existing space is minimized.
- Outsource those functions that are only needed sporadically, are too costly based on use, or take up excess space versus benefits to be derived from being on-site.

- Maximize the amount of current liabilities such as accounts and taxes payable to the extent possible without sacrificing good business practices by:
  ❏ Paying vendors within the range of their credit terms, but not before.
  ❏ Maximize the concept of disbursement float when paying vendors such as paying on the due date, mailing slowly, using the Federal Reserve clearing system, and calculating the vendor's processing float.
  ❏ Negotiate effectively with vendors so that the amount paid is the lowest possible, considering such things as discounts, payment periods, monthly statements versus individual invoices, finance charges, and so on.
  ❏ Consider paying vendors at the time of receipt where effective vendor negotiations make this practice the most economical.
  ❏ Eliminate or reduce the accounts payable function by direct payments to vendors where vendor prices and the costs savings dictate.

- Maximize the amount of net profits and increase in stockholders' equity by:
  ❏ Operating all functions and activities at the most economical levels. Remember that a dollar reduction in costs, all other things being equal, contributes dollar for dollar to the bottom line.

❏ Sell the right products, to the right customer, at the right time.

❏ Maximize the profitability of each sale through right pricing and costing.

❏ Calculate product costs by including all product-related costs and minimizing non-product overhead allocations.

❏ Calculate function costs (e.g., receiving, quality control, purchasing, accounts payable, and so on) as to those activities assignable to products and those that are non-value-added costs to be eliminated.

❏ Calculate additional customer costs so that customer profitabilty can be determined for future negotiations and pricing structure changes.

Customer Service Business

Not only does the company need to operate its functions and activities in the most economical, efficient, and effective manners, but it also needs to consider servicing its customers well if it desires to stay in business for the long term. Some best practices that might be considered in dealing with the company's customers include the following:

• Include the customer's needs in the company planning system.

• Consider customer requirements when considering product innovations or enhancements.

• Effectively negotiate with the customer so that the company is providing the right product, at the right time, with the highest quality.

• Coordinate with the customer so that prices can be provided at the lowest possible level that enables the company to make a fair profit.

• Provide pre-sale, during sale, and after-sale contact and service to the customer.

- Provide support services such as implementation, training, assistance, and so on as needed.
- Provide sufficient after-sale service so that the customer uses the company's products most effectively and is willing to buy more.
- Develop an organization structure to support the customer, not internal operations.

In addition, the study team should begin to accumulate specific detailed best practices which might be part of an internal or external benchmarking study or as part of the company's ongoing program of continuous improvements. Such practices should be brought to the attention of management and operations personnel in those functions appropriate to the best practice to be considered. Examples of such best practices include the following:

- "Catch me at my best" programs. Document an activity or process where an individual or group is caught performing the activity in the best manner.
- Maintaining the worth of the company through ongoing practices such as:
  - ❑ Employee relations
  - ❑ Cost reduction programs
  - ❑ Avoidance of regulatory problems
  - ❑ Capacity to increase good sales and revenues
  - ❑ Customer satisfaction and loyalty
  - ❑ Product reputation and quality
  - ❑ Planning and budget systems
  - ❑ Ability to increase productivity
  - ❑ Best practice and continuous improvement programs
- Continual searches for effective alternatives such as:
  - ❑ In-house versus outsourcing
  - ❑ Employees versus contractors
  - ❑ Sales personnel versus sales representatives or brokers
  - ❑ Salary versus commissions, bonuses, awards, and so on

- ❏ Self-responsibility versus other performed functions
- ❏ Functional control versus eliminating the function and the need for the control
- ❏ Employee reimbursements versus company debit or credit cards
- ❏ Conformity versus casual atmosphere
- ❏ Traditional accounts receivable versus factoring
- ❏ Isolationism versus partnering, alliances, cooperatives, and so on
- ❏ Direct sales versus other types of sales such as catalogs, fax, internet, distributors, and so on
- Developing an organizational structure that supports customer service:
  - ❏ Communicate—every employee should know exactly how the company operates and what they can do for the customer.
  - ❏ Emphasize what the customer values, what the customer is willing to pay for, and what the company is willing to provide.
  - ❏ Get around policies and procedures that limit real customer service.
  - ❏ Allow employees the necessary authority to do whatever it takes to satisfy the customer.
  - ❏ Hire the right people with customer service attitudes and personalities.
  - ❏ Make customer service a core value—from the top to the bottom.
  - ❏ Empower employees to do what is necessary to achieve customer service goals.
  - ❏ Solicit customer comments, share with others in the organization, and provide feedback to the customer.
  - ❏ Let employees know what is important to each type or individual customer.
  - ❏ Choose the right customers for your company—those that the company can service well.

- Establish a customer information file for all employees that includes such items as:
  - ❏ Customer contacts such as CEO, CFO, COO (chief operations officer), purchasing, manufacturing, engineering, accounting, personnel, and so on
  - ❏ Past sales as to product line, product, options, quantity, dollars, and so on
  - ❏ Past customer service contacts as to type of problem, solution, and so on
  - ❏ Current requests such as product enhancements, quality improvements, new products or options, and so on

FORMAL PRESENTATIONS

The external benchmarking team needs to focus their formal presentation on those areas with the greatest opportunities for improvement. Typically, these areas are first presented to host company internal management. It is a good practice to present study findings initially to operations personnel in the area under review. This allows for operations personnel to question any practices as to reasonableness in this situation, provide input as to how such a practice might best be implemented, correct any misconceptions as to present and proposed practices, and so on. Once the host company's operations and management personnel have reviewed, commented, and agreed or disagreed with any of the study team's findings, if desired or previously agreed the findings should be presented to the other study participants. Each of the other companies in the study should decide which personnel (management and operations) should attend such a joint presentation.

As a result of these formal presentations, the study team may decide that they have all of the information they need. Other times, the study team may realize that they need to gather additional information. In those instances, the study team may perform additional research and analyze and then report back to the group orally and/or in written format.

The study team should always identify the organization within the external benchmarking study group where ideas, suggestions, recommendations, or best practices emanated. In a joint presentation of all study participants, representatives from that organization can embellish or demonstrate how the process or practice works within their company and possibly identify how it could help other companies in the study.

In a formal presentation, oral or written, the study participants should have agreed in the original participation agreement as to whether companies and individuals are to be specifically identified or such identities are to remain unknown to all except the host company. Once such an agreement is made, all of those participating in the study must honor it. The participation agreement should also include the process and manner to report to all of those included in the study.

The study team must take extreme caution to ensure that reporting stays within the confines of the study participants included in the participation agreement. If other organizations outside of these study participants have been included in the study for research, comparison, analysis or some other purpose, the study team must make clear to them what study results they can expect to receive. This outside reporting must be consistent with the terms of the participation agreement as agreed by the study participants.

Formal presentations and reporting can be done on a progress basis as the external benchmarking study unfolds, as well as a final formal report at the end of the study. Progress reporting allows for best practices to be implemented as the study progresses.

FINAL REPORTS

The last step in the external benchmarking study is to prepare one final report for the host company internal management showing the study participants and detailed study results, and one for other company study participant management showing summary results without identifying study participants (unless all participants agree to sharing their identity). Typically, this final report becomes a summary of the external benchmarking study based on study findings, results, and additional comments made at any formal presentations.

Areas to consider in a external benchmarking study final report include:

- Data collection and results
- Analysis and interpretation of data
- Narratives—inconsistencies, steps taken and not taken
- Best practices and possible alternatives
- Cost versus benefit analysis
- Prioritization of opportunities for improvement
- Establishing new internal benchmarks after changes
- Future measurement and fine-tuning techniques
- What comes next
- Best practice presentations with comparisons between study participants
- Process comparisons between participants, with narratives of processes as required
- Recommendations as to best practices with descriptions
- Implementation procedures and concerns, including changes to be made, personnel involved, change over procedures, monitoring, and so on
- Other comments, narratives, conclusions, and addenda by the study team and other study participants

A suggested format for the external benchmarking study final report could include the following items:

- Background of the study
- Objectives and mission of study
- Scope of study
- Approach
- Personnel involved and their participation
- Study participants—description, characteristics, similarities, and differences

- Study participant comments, suggestions, and recommendations
- Relevant notes and comments from any formal presentations
- Summary of findings, conclusions, and opportunities
- Benchmarking results—narrative and graphics
- Opportunities for improvements
- Identification of unique and cutting-edge concepts
- Cost versus benefit analysis
- Recommendations for implementation
- Implementation plan
- Where to go from here
- Additional comments from study participants
- Appendices—statistical analysis, summary of results, graphs, charts, process detail, and so on
- Thank-you statement to each of the study team members and the study participants

SUMMARY: EXTERNAL BENCHMARKING PROCESS

The external benchmarking process focuses on developing learning organizations which are willing to remove the blinders from existing mental models that prevent the company from implementing a program of continuous improvement. When the organization realizes through benchmarking that it may not be doing things the way it should be (doing the right thing the right way), it must be willing to respond with action and growth—not denial.

Once the benchmarking concept takes hold within the company, the company should begin to implement continuous improvements by looking at methods, policies, and practices—learning from its own internal operations and personnel, and from external sources such as outside organizations (competitors, non-competitors, and industry and functional authorities), and consultants, specialists, and experts. Benchmarking is not a one-time company-wide or functional study, but a continuous process of improvement. The company's goal is to set the benchmarking system in motion through the performance of a benchmarking study—internal and/or external. The successful performance of the benchmarking study enables the company and its personnel, both management and operations personnel, to become a learning organization by leaving behind the residual capability of identifying and implementing continuous improvements and best practices.

An all-encompassing benchmarking process, which includes the elements of both internal and external benchmarking procedures, consists of four phases:

1. **Internal benchmarking study or assessment of current internal practices.** This study provides the starting point yardsticks, identifies performance drivers and constraints, and determines the critical areas for improvement. Internal benchmarking can provide comparisons to good business practices, standards of good principles, documented industry standards, and/or variable individuals or groups doing the same tasks or activities within the company. Internal benchmarking allows the company to become the best it can without the necessity of bringing outside companies into the benchmarking study.

   Although the company will miss the differing perspectives of these other organizations and possible best practices, it avoids the need to share its operations with the others. If the company desires to look for further improvements outside of the company through the conduct of an external benchmarking study, the internal benchmarking process should place them in a position where it looks as favorable as possible compared to others. Often, a smaller company or one with proprietary procedures can accomplish sufficient results through internal benchmarking alone. The company may decide that elaborate and costly external benchmarking procedures will produce minimal additional results.

2. **External benchmarking data-gathering procedures.** This phase begins with a clear definition of the purpose and goals of the external benchmarking study. Based on such

clearly defined goals, the benchmarking team develops data collection tools (questionnaires and interview goals and questions) and identifies other information sources such as books, periodicals, databases, web sites, experts, and so on.

The team also searches for and identifies appropriate benchmarking participant companies, groups, and individuals. The host company develops an external benchmarking team consisting of some of its employees (from management and operations), personnel from other company participants, and outsiders such as consultants and advisors. The benchmark team then performs the work steps to determine the different manners in which each company participant performs the functions and activities included in the benchmarking study. This is the field work or doing phase of the external benchmarking study.

3. **Data analysis phase** begins when the external benchmarking study data collection ends. This phase consists of the review and analysis of quantitative and qualitative data collected, leading to the identification and prioritization of performance gaps. The company learns what it is doing right the right way—and what it is doing wrong (doing the wrong things or doing the right things the wrong way). This is the phase where mental models are questioned and discarded, movement starts, and learning begins.

4. **Implementation or action phase** moving toward best practices. Comparing the company's performance to others may be heartening—gloating where the company's performance surpasses others; denying where the company's performance is less than others. However, scoring the company's performance is not the objective of benchmarking—making changes by implementing best practices and positive improvements is the real objective. As a result of the external benchmarking study, the company should develop an ongoing program of continuous improvement that pushes it toward best practices. Implementation of best practices becomes the responsibility of the entire organization

including top management, other management, operations personnel, implementation team, and other stakeholders. It is not a one-time implementation effort, but a continuous process of improvement—searching for best practices in all areas and practices of the company at all times.

Benchmarking procedures allow a company to compare their performance with internal standards of best practice, to make improvements, and then to compare this new level of performance to other companies' procedures to identify the operational practices that work best and then to implement such practices. Many internal managers are also using benchmarking to make their operations the best possible—and to ensure that they are doing everything possible to maintain their operations in the most economical, efficient, and effective manner. The benchmarking process then is a continual hunt for opportunities for positive improvements.

Every company has some areas that operate at less than optimum. By identifying the performance gaps between present and desired best practices, the company can work toward implementing procedures leading to excellence. In this manner, the company continually searches for competitive advantages that will make them the best possible. Benchmarking is a relentless and continuous process that enables the company to be the best they can and to stay that way.

An external benchmarking study example of the accounting function as part of a business cycle is documented below. It walks the reader through a representative external benchmarking study.

EXTERNAL BENCHMARKING STUDY EXAMPLE: ACCOUNTING FUNCTION AS PART OF A BUSINESS CYCLE

Introduction

Internal and external benchmarking are effective processes to look at the host company's and other company's operations to measure current processes and identify performance gaps. A thorough under-standing of such performance gaps enables company and depart-mental management to seize these opportunities for improvement. There has always been a demand—perhaps more so today—to decrease costs and improve product, service, and customer quality directed toward increasing profits. The accounting and finance func-tions historically have been the ones on whom company manage-ment have counted to provide and analysis financial data to control costs and increase profits. Ironically, rather than viewing these accounting functions as helping to achieve these goals, many com-panies see the accounting function as overhead (in many cases unnecessary costs) and are constantly moving to cut these costs. Benchmarking can assist in reducing non-value-added accounting function costs, while increasing the quality of providing accounting and financial value-added services.

Choosing What to Study

The external benchmarking study of the accounting and financial functions can be examined in a number of ways, such as:

- Functional—accounting, computer processing, treasury, reporting, and so on
- Process—accounts payable, accounts receivable, payroll, gen-eral ledger, budget, cash management, and so on
- Industry—manufacturing, retailing, banking, wholesaling, distribution, and so on
- Business cycle—based on the concept of closed loop activities such as:
  - ❏ Sales cycle—sales order, shipping, billing, accounts receiv-able, and collections
  - ❏ Purchase cycle—purchase requisition, purchasing, receiv-ing, vendor invoicing, accounts payable, cash disbursements
  - ❏ Payroll and labor distribution cycle—time and job verifi-cation, data entry, payroll and labor distribution process-ing, pay distribution, and record keeping.

❏ General ledger and financial statement cycle—subsystem data collection, journal entries, general ledger posting, and financial reporting

❏ Cost accounting cycle—material/labor/overhead data collection, computer processing, operating reports, off-line action, reporting by task, job, and period (e.g., daily, weekly, monthly)

I believe that accounting functions really can not be isolated on a linear basis from those other functions (e.g., sales, manufacturing, purchasing) that are supported and integrated with the specific accounting function. It is this thinking that has allowed such accounting functions to be cut back drastically in many organizations to the detriment of supported operating functions as noted above. In reality, a business operates in a circular or cyclical basis as shown above, with each component of the cycle equally as important. Therefore, to most effectively benchmark one of the accounting functions, it is best to look at it as part of its business cycle. We reviewed the purchase cycle as part of an internal benchmarking study in Chapter 2 and noted many areas for internal improvements. For the purposes of our external benchmarking example, we will look at the purchase cycle once again. In reality, we would select the business cycle for external benchmarking based on the identification of criticalness and priority ranking.

Developing the Benchmarking Team

The first decision in external benchmarking is selecting and developing the benchmarking team, especially a study manager who should be responsible for:

- Managing the study—developing the plan, assigning tasks, controlling activities, and results
- Obtaining ongoing top management commitment and support
- Coordinating periodic status reporting

The study manager can be one individual from the function under study, or from another area (or an internal individual skilled in benchmarking), or an outside consultant, or a combination of these personnel. Many times it is good practice to share study management responsibilities with those removed from the function in question. Other types of personnel that might be needed are researchers, data collectors, reviewers and analyzers, interviewers, operational reviewers, functional specialists, oral presenters, internal and external experts, and implementers.

When looking for members of the benchmarking team, the company should consider those possessing the following attributes:

- The ability to spot the trouble—to look at a given situation and quickly determine what is getting in the way
- The ability to identify the critical areas and related performance drivers
- The ability to place oneself in management's position, to analyze the problem, and ask questions from management's perspective
- The skill to effectively communicate study results—oral and written—with various organizational levels
- Analytical ability—to analyze a situation and identify the cause of the situation, not the symptom
- Problem-solving skills—to be able to analyze a problem situation and determine what needs to be done to correct it in a practical and reasonable way
- Good business judgment and common sense—to be able to identify doing the right thing and keep it that way
- Specific task skills—such as interviewing, presentation, researching, data collection, and interpretation
- Understanding of good business practices and a strategic business perspective
- Interpersonal skills—the ability to work well with other study team members as well as with management and operations personnel

- Systems orientation—the ability to understand the interrelationship between organizational functions and how they need to work together
- Understanding of change—the factors of resistance to change and the ability to effect positive change working with others

Use of Outside Assistance

The external benchmarking study team is not limited to using only internal company personnel when conducting their benchmarking study. As the study team is working toward identifying and implementing best practices for the company, they may find that adequate personnel with the above attributes do not exist within the company. This may force them to go outside the company to find the right individuals. The external benchmarking study and its results will only be as good as the personnel conducting the study. It is usually well worth the cost of using outsiders (but used judiciously) as such individuals can:

- Bring previous benchmarking experience to the study
- Help identify benchmarking participants
- Exercise expertise in specific areas such as accounting, manufacturing, sales, engineering, and so on
- Identify innovative approaches (many times learned from others) to consider
- Locate additional sources of information
- Quickly identify and eliminate areas of minimal benefit
- Provide entrée to additional resources and study participants
- Work independently and objectively within the company, without being affected by organizational constraints and power struggles and other internal tasks
- Provide knowledge of involvement in previous benchmarking studies conducted for others

Identifying Study Participants

Selecting the right external benchmarking participants is extremely critical to the success of the study. To be part of the study, the host company could merely select other companies known to them or which are willing to be part of it. A better and more successful approach is to carefully screen potential participants for suitability to the host company, looking at such factors as:

- Relative size in sales dollars, number of employees, locations and facilities, types of processes, and so on
- Type of organization, such as small closely held business, public corporation, division of larger entity, and so on
- Processes such as local manufacturing, original equipment manufacturer (OEM), service provider, reseller, distributor, or a combination of these processes
- Geographical considerations such as location, other locations, territory covered, domestic and/or international
- Industry similarities such as one product, multi-product or divisions, major/minor focus, and so on

When determining appropriate benchmarking study participants, the host company could consider many potential companies (or very few). In most situations, the host company will not be able to determine the best ones until after the study has been completed. The number of study participants selected is often a factor of the time and budget available to conduct the study and the severity of the desired results. Within these constraints, typically, the more companies that can be included in the study, the better the results.

The few companies selected for inclusion in the external benchmarking study constitute only a small number of the total population—whether competitive, industry, or best-in-class. However, the next time an external benchmarking study is conducted, the host company can include other companies that might be equally or more appropriate—making benchmarking a continual process. To start with, the study team need not look for the ultimate best participants, but for those who are better than the host company in the areas under review. Keep in mind that it is possible to learn something meaningful from each and every study participant, those who are better than the host company and those who are worse. We use three participants for case study purposes.

Prioritizing Activities

One of the first steps for the external benchmarking team is the identification and prioritization of those activities related to the purchase cycle to include in the study. These should be the most critical areas to the company as identified in the internal benchmark operational review as well as feedback from the external study participants via such things as surveys, interviews, and group brainstorming. For our case study purposes we have identified the following activities:

- Organizational issues
  - ❏ Authority, responsibility, and management
  - ❏ Personnel functions
  - ❏ Purchasing policies
  - ❏ Budget and actual costs
- Purchasing function
  - ❏ Purchase requisitioning
  - ❏ Purchase ordering
  - ❏ Vendor relations, negotiations, analysis
  - ❏ Open purchase orders and expediting
  - ❏ Purchasing value analysis
- Receiving function
  - ❏ Open receipt control
  - ❏ Receiving procedures
  - ❏ Receiving inspection
  - ❏ Routing procedures
- Accounts payable and cash disbursements functions
  - ❏ Accounts payable processing
  - ❏ Open accounts payable control
  - ❏ Vendor payment processing

❏ Cash disbursement processing
❏ Record-keeping and analysis

Developing the External Benchmarking Questionnaire

As discussed previously, one of the most important elements of the external benchmarking study is the participant questionnaire. The main purpose of the questionnaire is to reduce large amounts of data into categories or areas that can be compared more easily. The questions are developed by the study team directed toward those areas defined as most critical. Each question attempts to focus on one factor of an area to be measured. The questions are designed to provide objective answers and data relative to the performance criteria in question and to identify unique methods and best practices.

The external benchmarking team—host company internal members, outside consultants, and study participant members—develops and field-tests the questionnaire. Each question is probed as to its objectivity, purpose, data to be provided, closed-endedness, and so on. Typically, the questionnaire is designed for each individual benchmarking study, although questions can be used from previous (or published) studies if they are appropriate to the current situation.

A sample questionnaire related to the purchase cycle was shown in Exhibit 5.3. We will be using this same questionnaire for the purposes of our case example and for summarizing the responses from study participants.

Compiling the Data

Once each participant (the host company and the other study participants) has returned the questionnaires to the study team, the study team needs to review and analyze each questionnaire for inappropriate, misleading, or inadequate responses. This usually requires going back to the respondent for clarification—either by phone or personal site visit. If possible, it is good practice to have one individual or more assigned to each participant, with each participant having an assigned benchmarking coordinator. It is by effectively working together with all study participants that the members of the study team will be able to finalize all responses for each participant.

Once the study team is satisfied with the legitimacy of each of the participants' questionnaire responses, the next step is to summarize the responses of all study participants, including the host company, on one document for analysis purposes. This analysis helps to identify best practices among study participants in total and by individual area for presentation to host company management and operations personnel and all study participants. Such recording summarization can be done quite easily by recording each participant's responses directly on the questionnaire document itself.

The benchmarking team should then individually and collectively (normally in a brainstorming session) identify best practices and summarize process comparisons for those areas determined to be most critical for presentation to management. The sample external benchmarking questionnaire showing a summary of questionnaire responses for the host company and the three study participants is shown in Exhibit 5.7.

Exhibit 5.7 External Benchmarking Questionnaire

Purchase Cycle: Purchasing, Receiving, Accounts Payable Functions

Summary of Questionnaire Responses

Participants: Us, Company A, Company B, Company C

I. ORGANIZATIONAL ISSUES

    A. How are these functions organized?
       Hierarchical (H), Vertical (V), Integrated (I), Other (O)
       Response: Us = H
                   A = V
                   B = H
                   C = H

(continues)

Exhibit 5.7 *(Continued)*

B. To whom does each function report?
   Response: Us = Purchasing: VP/Operations; Receiving: Plant Manager; Payables: Controller
   A = Purchasing: VP/Purchasing; Receiving: VP/Purchasing; Payables: VP/ Finance
   B = Purchasing: VP/Manufacturing; Receiving: VP/Manufacturing; Payables: VP/Finance
   C = Purchasing: President; Receiving: Plant Manager; Payables: President

C. Who manages each function?
   Response: Us = Purchasing: Manager; Receiving: Manager; Payables: Supervisor
   A = Purchasing: Supervisor; Receiving: Supervisor; Payables: Supervisor
   B = Purchasing: Director; Receiving: Plant Manager; Payables: Manager
   C = Purchasing: Supervisor; Receiving: Supervisor; Payables: Supervisor

D. How many employees in each function?
   Response: Us = Purchasing 7, Receiving 3, Accounts Payable 2
   A = Purchasing 5, Receiving 2, Accounts Payable 2
   B = Purchasing 9, Receiving 5, Accounts Payable 4
   C = Purchasing 3, Receiving 1, Accounts Payable 1

E. What are your major purchasing policies (e.g., dollar limit for central purchasing)?
   Response: Us= $50
   A = $400
   B = $200
   C = $500

F. What is the total budget and actual allocations for each function?
   Response: Us=Purchasing: $320,000/ $367,000; Receiving: $ 64,000/ $ 86,000; Accounts Payable: $ 46,000/$ 58,000
   A = Purchasing: $180,000/$164,000; Receiving: $ 42,000/ $ 36,000; Accounts Payable: $ 34,000/$ 28,000
   B = Purchasing: $348,000/$326,000; Receiving: $ 87,000/ $ 82,000; Accounts Payable: $ 54,000/$ 48,000
   C = Purchasing: $126,000/$147,000; Receiving: $ 38,000/ $ 36,000; Accounts Payable: $ 28,000/$ 24,000

Exhibit 5.7 *(Continued)*

G. Do you have functional job descriptions for each position?
Response: Us = No
A = Yes
B = No
C = No

II. PURCHASING FUNCTION

A. *Purchase Requisitions (PRs)*

1. How are PRs prepared? Manual form, computer processed, automatic from planning system?
Response: Us = Manual form
A = computer
B = computer
C = computer

2. How many PRs were processed in the past fiscal year? Total company.
Response: Us = 34,000
A = 18,000
B = 22,000
C = 14,600

3. What percent of PRs were returned to users for correction?
Response: Us = 6.4%
A = 2.8%
B = 4.3%
C = 1.6%

4. Do you use computer processing to integrate and process PRs to purchase orders?
Response: Us = No
A = Yes
B = Yes
C = Yes

5. On average, how quickly can you process a PR to a PO?
Response: Us = three days
A = one day
B = two days
C ≤ one day

(continues)

Exhibit 5.7   *(Continued)*

---

6. Do you provide on-line access to open PRs to operating departments and individuals?
   Response: Us = No
   A = Yes
   B = No
   C = Yes

B. *Purchase Orders (POs)*

1. How are POs prepared? Manual, computer, automatic from other systems?
   Response: Us = Manual
   A = computer
   B = computer
   C = Automatic/computer

2. How many POs were processed in the past fiscal year? Total Company.
   Response: Us = 30,000
   A = 14,000
   B = 19,500
   C = 12,200

3. Do you use electronic data transfer (EDT) for any POs?
   Response: Us = No
   A = Yes/10%
   B = No
   C = Yes/30%

4. On average, how quickly can you process a PO?
   Response: Us = three days
   A = one day
   B = one day
   C ≤ one day

5. What is your average number of POs processed? By day, by employee?
   Response: Us = 125/60+
   A = 55/25+
   B = 75/25+
   C = 45/45+

6. Do you produce a hard copy PO? How many parts?
   Response: Us = Yes, six part
   A = No

Exhibit 5.7   *(Continued)*

B = Yes, four part
C = Yes, four part

7. Do you provide on-line access to open POs to operating departments and individuals?
   Response: Us = No
              A = Yes
              B = Yes
              C = Yes

8. What is your cost to process a purchase order?
   Response: Us = $75
              A = $42
              B = $56
              C = $28

9. When was the last time this cost was calculated?
   Response: Us = recent
              A = two years
              B = four years
              C = one year

10. Is the cost to process a purchase order used in the formula to calculate reorder quantities?
    Response: Us = Yes
               A = No
               B = Yes
               C = No

11. What is your minimal amount to process a purchase through central purchasing?
    Response: Us = $50
               A = $400
               B = $200
               C = $500

Describe other systems for purchases under this amount.

Response: Us = None
           A = Direct purchase
           B = None
           C = Direct purchase cards

(continues)

Exhibit 5.7 *(Continued)*

C. *Vendor Relations, Negotiations, Analysis*

1. What is the total number of vendors in your system?
   Response: Us = 587
             A = 264
             B = 349
             C = 182

2. Are your vendors coded by type of commodity class?
   Response: Us = Yes
             A = Yes
             B = No
             C = Yes

3. Can you provide a summary of vendors by commodity class?
   Response: Us = Yes
             A = Yes
             B = No
             C = Yes

4. How often do you negotiate with vendors? Each purchase, monthly, annually, other.
   Response: Us = by exception
             A = annual
             B = annual
             C = each purchase

5. How many vendors make up approximately 80 percent of your total purchases?
   Response: Us = 128
             A = 68
             B = 146
             C = 42

6. Do you use long-term contracts or blanket purchase orders to lock in price, quality, and prompt deliveries?
   Response: Us = rarely
             A = major vendors
             B = rarely
             C = where possible

7. Do you integrate raw material purchases into your production schedule?
   Response: Us = No

Exhibit 5.7 *(Continued)*

A = Yes
B = Yes
C = Yes

8. Do you maintain vendor analysis statistics?
   Response: Us = No
   A = Yes, but no quality data
   B = No
   C = Yes, plus history data

9. Are company individuals assigned contact responsibility for major vendors?
   Response: Us = No
   A = No
   B = Yes
   C = No

10. How often are long-term purchase contracts renegotiated?
    Response: Us = rarely
    A = annual
    B = rarely
    C = ongoing

11. Do you have an ongoing process for identification of potential vendors?
    Response: Us = No
    A = No
    B = No
    C = Yes

12. How many vendors have you added during the past year?
    Response: Us = 57
    A = 24
    B = 35
    C = 12

13. How many vendors have you deleted during the past year?
    Response: Us = 68
    A = 18
    B = 27
    C = 8

(continues)

Exhibit 5.7 *(Continued)*

D. *Open Purchase Order Control and Expediting*

1. How many POs, on average, are open at any one time?
   Response: Us = 900+
         A = 680
         B = 840
         C = 360

2. Are open POs part of an integrated computer system?
   Response: Us = No
         A = Yes
         B = Yes
         C = Yes

3. Are open POs reported for expediting via this system?
   Response: Us = No
         A = Yes
         B = Yes
         C = Yes

4. Do you use automatic data transmission for open PO expediting?
   Response: Us = No
         A = Yes
         B = No
         C = No

5. Do you expedite on a personal contact basis?
   Response: Us = Yes
         A = No
         B = Yes
         C = No

6. On average, how many POs are being expedited at one time?
   Response: Us = 80+
         A = 48
         B= 37
         C = 22

7. On average, how many expedited POs require follow-up calls?
   Response: Us = 40+
         A = 34
         B = 25
         C = 8

Exhibit 5.7   *(Continued)*

___

  E. *Purchasing Value Analysis*

  1. Does the purchasing function have authority to question
      purchases?
      Response: Us = No
      A = Yes
      B = Yes/No
      C = Yes

  2. Do they have authority to question?
      Response: Us = No
      A = All but necessity
      B = not RM
      C = All

  3. Can they initiate or process changes?
      Response: Us = No
      A = Yes
      B = Yes
      C = Yes

III. RECEIVING FUNCTION

  1. On average, what is the total number of open receipts? POs,
      items?
      Response: Us = 800+/2600+
      A = 380/500+
      B = 270/400+
      C = 580/800+

  2. What types of items or commodity classes are received by this
      function?
      Response: Us = all
      A = manufacturing only
      B = all but office
      C = manufacturing

  3. What types of items or commodity classes are received by another
      manner? Describe.
      Response: Us = None
      A = direct by user
      B = office by user
      C = direct by user

(continues)

Exhibit 5.7 *(Continued)*

---

4. Are open PO receipts part of an integrated computer system?
   Response: Us = No
   A = Yes
   B = Yes
   C = Yes

5. On average, how many receipts are processed in a day?
   Response: Us = 150+
   A = 80+
   B = 110+
   C = 46

6. Do all such receipts come to a central receiving area? Describe exceptions.
   Response: A = Yes
   B = Yes
   C = Yes

7. Does the user receive any items directly? What types? Describe procedure.
   Response: Us = No
   A = other than manufacturing
   B = office items
   C = other than manufacturing

8. Are receipts processed by some form of on-line computer system?
   Response: Us = No
   A = Yes
   B = Yes
   C = Yes

9. Are any receipts processed on a manually prepared form basis?
   Response: Us = All
   A = No
   B= No
   C = No

10. Are receipts part of an integrated computer system?
    Response: Us = No
    A = Yes
    B = No
    C = Yes

Exhibit 5.7 *(Continued)*

---

11. Do you have a receiving inspection function? Inspect all items or by exception?
    Response: Us = Yes, all
    A = Yes, all
    B = Yes, manufacturing only
    C = No

12. On average, how quickly are items routed to users?
    Response: Us = next day
    A = same day
    B = same day
    C = within the hour

13. Do you use Just in Time (JIT) practices for raw materials?
    Response: Us = No
    A = Yes
    B = No
    C = Yes

14. Are these raw material receipts integrated with your production schedule?
    Response: Us = No
    A = Yes
    B = No
    C = Yes

15. Do you have documented receiving procedures?
    Response: Us = No
    A = No
    B = Yes
    C = No

16. Are open receipts reconciled to open purchase orders? Computer or manual? How often? Percent of errors?
    Response: Us = No
    A = No
    B = Yes
    C = No

17. Do you use bar coding in processing your receipts?
    Response: Us = No
    A = Yes
    B = Yes
    C = Yes

(continues)

Exhibit 5.7 *(Continued)*

---

18. What percent of your total receipts are bar coded?
    Response: Us = None
              A = 20+%
              B = 20+%
              C = 60+%

IV. ACCOUNTS PAYABLE

A. *Accounts Payable Processing*

1. On what basis and percents of total payments do you pay vendors?

   a. Prepay at time of order?
      Response: Us = None
                A = RM, 20%
                B = None
                C = RM, 30%

   b. Payment upon receipt?
      Response: Us = None
                A = RM, 10%
                B = None
                C = RM, 40%

   c. Payment with invoice/receipt within discount terms?
      Response: Us = 30%
                A = 50%
                B = 60%
                C = 30%

   d. Payment with invoice/receipt within 30 days?
      Response: Us = 70%/discount
                A = 20%/discount
                B = 40%/discount
                C = 0%

2. How often do you process accounts payable for payment?
   Response: Us = twice a week
             A = weekly
             B = weekly
             C = twice a month

3. Do you make any exceptions between payment periods?
   Response: Us = Yes
             A = Yes

Exhibit 5.7 *(Continued)*

B = Yes

C = No

4. Do you provide for off-line manual vendor payments?
   Response: Us = Yes

   A = Yes

   B = Yes

   C = No

5. What is the amount of new accounts payable at any time?
   Number of payments/total sums?
   Response: Us = 800/260,000

   A = 560/180,000

   B = 500/168,000

   C = 320/126,000

6. Is accounts payable processing part of an integrated
   computer system?
   Response: Us = No

   A = Yes

   B = Yes

   C = Yes

7. What is the amount of annual payments? Number of
   payments? Total dollars?
   Response: Us = 26,000, $4,800,000

   A = 16,000, $2,200,000

   B = 18,000, $3,300,000

   C = 12,000, $2,800,000

B. *Open Accounts Payable Control*

1. Are open accounts payable part of an integrated computer
   system?
   Response: Us = No

   A = Yes

   B = Yes

   C = Yes

2. How often do you process payments?
   Response: Us = twice a week

   A = weekly

   B = weekly

   C = monthly

(continues)

Exhibit 5.7 *(Continued)*

3. Is there a policy to take vendor discounts? Within/at the discount period?
   Response: Us = Yes/Yes
   A = Yes/Yes
   B = Yes/Yes
   C = Yes/Yes

4. On average, what is the amount of open accounts payable? Number of invoices/total sums?
   Response: Us = 1400/620,000
   A = 880/340,000
   B = 940/280,000
   C = 480/210,000

5. Are open accounts payable accessible on an on-line basis?
   Response: Us = No
   A = Yes/AP
   B = Yes/AP
   C = Yes/All

C. *Vendor Payment Processing*

1. Do you provide a pre-payment listing of due bills prior to processing? On screen? Listing only? Both options?
   Response: Us = No
   A = Both
   B = Both
   C = Both

2. Can an authorized individual select bills for payment? Manual? On-line? Additions? Deletions? Changes?
   Response: Us = Manual
   A = All
   B = All
   C = All

3. Can an authorized individual determine the dollar amount for total payment? What is basis for selection?
   Response: Us = Yes/money available
   A = Yes/money to be paid
   B = Yes/money to be paid
   C = Yes/money to be paid

Exhibit 5.7 *(Continued)*

---

4. How often do you process checks for payment? Do you hold to that schedule? How many times did you go off that schedule last year?
   Response: Us = twice a week/yes/never
                 A = weekly/yes/4 times
                 B = weekly/yes/8 times
                 C = monthly/yes/never

5. Do you automatically combine vendor invoices into one payment?
   Response: Us = No
                 A = Yes
                 B = Yes
                 C = Yes

6. Do you provide detail as to what invoices are paid?
   Response: Us = No
                 A = Yes
                 B = Yes
                 C = Yes

7. Do you reconcile vendor statements to individual invoices?
   Response: Us = Yes
                 A = No
                 B = Yes
                 C = No

8. Do you ignore vendor statements and pay only by invoice?
   Response: Us = No
                 A = Yes
                 B = No
                 C = Yes

9. Do you automatically net vendor debits against payments?
   Response: Us = No
                 A = Yes
                 B = Yes
                 C = Yes

10. On average, what is the amount of vendor debits? Number of debits? Total amount?
   Response: Us = 140/$6,000+
                 A = 24/$1,200
                 B = 48/$3,800
                 C = 8/$350   *(continues)*

Exhibit 5.7 *(Continued)*

---

11. Once selected, are checks with payment detail automatically processed?
    Response: Us = No
    A = Yes
    B = Yes
    C = Yes

12. What is your cost per payment?
    Response: Us = $48
    A = $38
    B = $44
    C = $26

13. What is your cost per processing cycle?
    Response: Us = $800+ twice a week
    A = $580 weekly
    B = $660 weekly
    C = $370 monthly

14. On average, how many payments do you process at one time? Per process run? Per month? Annually?
    Response: Us = 350/2,800/34,000
    A = 350/1,400/16,800
    B = 420/1,680/20,200
    C = 1,200/1,200/14,400

D. *Cash Disbursement Processing*

1. Are payments as processed automatically sent to the vendor? Electronic data transfer? Mail?
    Response: Us = Mail
    A = Mail/EDT 10%
    B = Mail
    C = Mail/EDT 60%

2. How often do you process cash disbursements?
    Response: Us = Twice a week
    A = Weekly
    B = Weekly
    C = Monthly

3. On average, what are the number of checks written? By process? Monthly? Annual?
    Response: Us = 350/2,800/34,000
    A = 280/1,120/13,000

Exhibit 5.7 *(Continued)*

B = 340/1,360/16,000
C = 960/960/11,000

4. Do you combine payments by vendor? On what basis?
   Response: Us = No
   A = Yes/Due dates by latest discount
   B = Yes/Due dates by earliest discount
   C = Yes/Due Dates by latest discount

5. On what basis do you process payment? Receipt of items?
   Invoice? Both? Other?
   Response: Us = Both
   A = Both
   B = Both
   C = Both

6. Do you use a remote bank location?
   Response: Us = No
   A = No
   B = No
   C = Yes

7. Do you use any methods to slow the receipt of the payment to
   the vendor? Describe.
   Response: Us = No
   A = Yes/mail end of day
   B = No
   C = Remote mail

8. What is your cost per check disbursement? What is your cost
   per disbursement cycle?
   Response: Us = $1.12/$392
   A = $.78/$220
   B = $.94/$320
   C = $.66/$634

9. How many times have checks been processed late in the last
   year? Sent out late?
   Response: Us = 2/2
   A = 4/7
   B = 6/13
   C = 12/12

(continues)

Exhibit 5.7 *(Continued)*

10. What percent of checks have reported errors upon receipt? Hours spent in correcting?
    Response: Us = 12%/180
    A = 7%/67
    B = 9%/86
    C = 4%/12

11. Do you provide electronic data transfer for vendor payments?
    Response: Us = No
    A = Yes
    B = Yes
    C = No

12. Is timeliness of payment considered as a factor in vendor price negotiations?
    Response: Us = No
    A = No
    B = Yes
    C = No

E. *Record-Keeping and Analysis*

1. What records do you keep for each payment?
   Response: Us = All
   A = All but voucher
   B = All
   C = All but PO and invoice

2. What type of analysis do you do relative to payments?
   Response: Us = none
   A = pay/vendors
   B = pay/vendors
   C = all plus float period

3. Are there other records/analysis that you do? Describe.
   Response: Us = none
   A = last purchase/price
   B = None
   C = competitive analysis

4. What report options do you provide? Standard in software/custom defined/user?
   Response: Us = standard
   A = custom/user
   B = custom/user
   C = custom/user

Exhibit 5.7 *(Continued)*

---

5. What software do you use for these functions?
   Response: Us = low end
   A = medium
   B = medium
   C = high end

6. What computer hardware configuration do you use?
   Response: Us = PC net (3 stations)
   A = PC net (8 stations)
   B = PC net (6 stations)
   C = PC net (22 stations)

The external benchmarking study team is aware that data reported via such a questionnaire process may be unclear and misleading due to:

- Methods of data gathering
- Misunderstanding of terminology
- Attitude of person providing the data
- Completeness and accuracy of data base
- Misunderstanding of data requested

Due to these possibilities of data inaccuracies, the benchmarking team will usually thoroughly analyze the data provided prior to the identification for best practices and process comparisons. As the study team typically relies on the data provided (by various participant management and operations personnel) in determining their conclusions, they need to determine whether any data elements require further back-up from the participant as to methods of estimation, formulas used, and calculation routines. Normally, a range of results presents itself, so that if one participant is way off it becomes readily apparent. This allows the study team to easily identify those items out of the range and contact that participant for further review and resubmission. A sample of identification of best practices is shown in Exhibit 5.8, and a sample of process comparisons is shown in Exhibit 5.9. based on questionnaire responses.

Exhibit 5.8 Analysis of Questionnaire Responses: Identification of Best Practices

1. *Time to Process a Purchase Requisition to a Purchase Order*

Company	Time	Rank
Us	3 days	4
A	1 day	2
B	2 days	3
C	<1 day	1 (best practice)

2. *Dollar Limit for Central Purchasing*

Company	Cost	Rank
Us	$ 50	4
A	400	2
B	200	3
C	500	1 (best practice)

3. *Cost to Process a Purchase Order*

Company	Cost	Rank
Us	$ 75	4
A	42	2
B	56	3
C	28	1 (best practice)

4. *Employees per Function*

Company	Number			Rank		
	PU	RC	AP	PU	RC	AP
Us	7	3	2	3	3	2
A	5	2	2	2	2	2
B	9	5	4	4	4	4
C	3	1	1	1	1	1 (best practice)

Exhibit 5.8   *(Continued)*

5. *Purchase Orders per Year*

Company	Number	Rank
Us	30,000	1
A	14,000	3
B	19,500	2
C	12,200	4 (best practice)

6. *Number of Vendors*

Company	Number	Rank
Us	587	1
A	264	3
B	349	2
C	182	4 (best practice)

7. *Vendors Added in Last Year*

Company	Number	Rank
Us	57	1
A	24	3
B	35	2
C	12	4 (best practice)

8. *Receipts Processed in a Day*

Company	Number	Rank
Us	150	1
A	80	3
B	110	2
C	46	4 (best practice)

(continues)

Exhibit 5.8 *(Continued)*

9. *Period for Processing Payments*

Company	Time	Rank
Us	Twice/Week	4
A	Weekly	2
B	Weekly	2
C	Monthly	1 (best practice)

10. *Cost per Payment/Per Check*

Company	Cost	Rank
Us	$48/1.12	4/4
A	38/0.78	2/2
B	44/0.94	3/3
C	26/0.66	1/1 (best practice)

Exhibit 5.9 Process Comparisons

Type of Process	Study Participant			
	Us	A	B	C
1. *Organization Structure*				
Integrated functions	No	No	No	No
Flat structure	No	Yes	No	Yes
High $ limit/low budget	No	Yes	No	Yes
2. *Manual versus Automated*				
EDP integration	No	Yes	Yes	Yes
Use of EDT	No	Yes	No	Yes
On-line access to data	No	Yes	Yes	Yes
3. *Functional Integration*				
RM to production schedule	No	Yes	Yes	Yes
PRs to budget system	No	No	No	No

Exhibit 5.9   *(Continued)*

Type of Process	Study Participant			
	Us	*A*	*B*	*C*
Purch/Rec/AP integration	No	Yes	Y/N	Y/N
Functional job descriptions	No	Yes	No	No
4. *Purchase Requisitions*				
Automated	No	Yes	Yes	Yes
Computer: PRs to POs	No	Yes	Yes	Yes
PR on-line access	No	Yes	No	Yes
5. *Purchase Orders*				
Automatic from other systems	No	No	No	Yes
Electronic data transfer	No	Y/10%	No	Y/30%
Hard copy purchase order	Y/6	No	Y/4	Y/4
6. *Vendor Analysis*				
Code by commodity class	Yes	Yes	No	Yes
Vendor analysis statistics	No	Yes	No	Yes
Identify potentials	No	No	No	Yes
7. *Purchase Value Analysis*				
Authority to question	No	Yes	Y/N	Yes
Initiate/process change	No	Yes	Yes	Yes
8. *Receiving Function*				
Central receiving area	Yes	Yes	Yes	Yes
On-line computer system	No	Yes	Yes	Yes
Bar coding	No	Y/20	Y/20	Y/60
9. *Accounts Payable*				
Prepay at order	No	Y/20	No	Y/30
Exceptions between pays	Yes	Yes	Yes	No
Prepayment listing	No	Yes	Yes	Yes
10. *Cash Disbursements*				
Combine vendor invoices	No	Yes	Yes	Yes
Detail for payments	No	Yes	Yes	Yes
Slow receipt methods	No	Yes	No	Yes

REVISITING CONTINUOUS IMPROVEMENTS

The benchmarking process, like the company itself, is always in constant change. The nature of the business, the necessary functions and operations, the use of personnel, customer requirements, and so on do, not remain static, but change constantly. Organizational and internal benchmarks must be continually revisited to ensure that they are still appropriate to move the company toward its desired results. The company's competition and industry are continually developing new best practices and raising the threshold of excellence. In addition, new innovations as to functional best-in-class practices are continually developed and implemented across industry lines, especially with the speed of technological changes. While the company has moved to meet or surpass a benchmark performance gap, the competitor or practice itself has improved so that a new benchmark gap has surfaced. There is also the possibility that new companies have emerged who have exploited an opportunity or developed a best practice that didn't previously exist. For all of these reasons and others, the company must continually revisit its perceived best practices in a company-wide program of continuous benchmarking and improvements.

> ### *We're Grasping, But We're Not Holding On*

The company needs to continually revisit their benchmarks and best practices to reinforce the effectiveness of its program for continuous improvements. For the learning organization to be most effective, organizational, internal, and external benchmarks must be currently maintained and perceived best practices must be analyzed and reviewed on an ongoing basis. All employees, management as well as operations personnel, should be responsible for such continual review and change. An indication of an effective learning organization is that all levels of personnel are responsible for such systems and practice changes. In an organization where self-motivated disciplined behavior is the rule, rather than control, this becomes an automatic expectation of each individual.

Organizational benchmarks which are typically the domain of top management may need to be reviewed frequently to re-assess the company's own goals as well as its changing position relative to its competitors and its industry. There are numerous external factors which may impact on the organization and a need for change:

- Competitor innovations—products, practices, marketing changes, and so on
- New external developments—technology, practices, economies, and so on
- Practice and process improvements—functions, activities, eliminations, and so on
- Organizational changes—structure, mental models, performance drivers, and so on
- Past identified best practices which can now be implemented

CONCLUSION

The internal and external benchmarking study can provide the identification of opportunities for improvement and best practices. However, this does not ensure that management or operations personnel will agree or that the organization will accept the findings. The benchmark study team must present their findings convincingly and persuasively so that the organization sees the benefit of implementing their recommendations. Without such an organizational acceptance, success will be limited.

> ## *Standing Still Is Losing Ground*

Normally, with systemic changes, such acceptance of new ideas and methods, particularly those that threaten prevalent mental models, takes time for effective change (if at all). The understanding of the internal and external benchmarking process is critical to the acceptance and ultimate success of implementation of the study team's benchmarking findings and recommendations.

As with any organizational or operational change, any individual—manager or staff employee—can be a potential roadblock to change. Those in positions of authority—and sometimes those without formal authority—can feel threatened by the change and find numerous reasons why the change should not be implemented. The will do what they can to prevent such change. Some of the things that these people should realize to lessen their resistance to change include the following:

- Benchmarking is an organizational and people process.
- Benchmarking data may be difficult to quantify. Comparisons between study participants indicate relative performance, not necessarily hard numeric data.
- Those critical areas represent the starting point for opportunities for improvement. There may be numerous other areas to be examined in the future as you develop your program for continuous improvement.
- Quantification of results may not always be possible. Many times benchmarking results in organizational or mental model changes which we know are positive but cannot be quantified.
- Benchmarking findings and recommendations often result in basic operating philosophy or practice (We've always done it that way) changes that may not be defined in terms of actual numeric payout.
- Benchmarking results should relate back to the organization's basic philosophy and strategy for operating (e.g., customer service and cash conversion) as well as their position in their competitive universe.
- Benchmarking is a tool to assist the organization to move toward its desired strategic position in a positive manner which continually stresses the adoption of best practices

and a program of continuous improvement in all areas of its operations.

- Benchmarking is a continual process, not a one-time study that requires the attention and participation of the entire organization from top management to entry level employees.
- The benchmarking study is the starting point in your program for positive change, continual implementation of best practice changes is the ending point.

The benchmarking process—both internal and external—may begin with a one-time study that results in the implementation of best practices. This initial study is really the starting point for benchmarking within the organization. As part of the benchmarking study, benchmarking concepts should be bred into each operational area. The residual capability of looking at operations for improvements should be ongoing. The benchmarking study thus becomes the beginning of the organization's program for continuous improvements. Benchmarking becomes an integral part of the organization's systems and operations.

Index

Index

Index

Index